1

A Global Perspective

***

SPIRITUALITY
FOR ALL

***

PRIMER-SIMPLE
INTERFAITH

***

MAN
and his
UNIVERSE

Dr. Abdul Rehman Abd

ISBN: 9798754520141

Book cover designed by: Hina

Price = $20

Dr. Abdul Rehman Abd

Allama Iqbal Global Forum, New York

Arehmanmd123@gmail.com

عبد ، لکھو در پہ ایسے "مرحبا ! خوش آمد ید"

دیکھ کر تختی تری محفل میں آئیں خاص و عام

In loving memory of

my Parents

in recognition of their being my inspiration

and their role in fostering in me, the

love for everything spiritual

***

CONTENTS

"I"

I existed as a spirit in a higher realm of life before this Earth came into being.
I Waited and took my turn to get here to have a brief Human experience.
Soon, I will go back home and be forever at peace.

AN OPEN MIND

Humans are created as independent thinkers. All of us have our opinions, sometimes wrapped up under a broader group opinion. All that is well and good because that seems to be the design of our world. However, we must realize and acknowledge that:

-Open mindedness is essential if one wants to change oneself for the better. No amount of rain can fill a pitcher unless the pitcher is upright, and its lid is open.

-There are multiple Organized religious or faith systems in the world, each believing firmly that they are right. Many humans don't believe in God or any other higher power. Every group claims to be well informed and has well educated intellectuals as their members.

-There are multiple sects and groups within every "Organized" religion or faith system. Opinion given by anyone in a particular religious or faith group may not represent the views of everyone in that group. Representations made in this book, therefore, are also to be viewed with that perspective and to be used as a catalyst for further learning.

-All of us are children of Adam and Eve. Our Creator is one. His message for all of us, is, and had to be the same. Did our Creator really want us to approach him differently based on when and where we lived our life and under what label? Have we cornered ourselves for too long, in such a way that we are incapable of connecting to our inner self with an open mind? Have we met our true being – the spiritual being, the "Self", that is our real and true identity.

-A significant number of us, may be non-believers as independent thinking youngsters and then young parents. With maturity, and by the time we become grandparents, most of us see the light and become believers. Irony is that by then, we have replaced ourselves with our independent thinking children and grandchildren. The grandchildren consider us irrelevant and ignore our counsel, and the cycle goes on.

-An attempt is hereby being made to invite the reader to increase awareness about each other's belief system with the aim of ensuring mutual respect and a harmonious interactions and relationship. Hopefully, this will inspire the reader for further learning and an open-minded healthy interfaith dialogue.

Life Story

Where are we headed and where have we been?
The narration we heard, is of a point in between.

کہاں جا رہے ہیں ، ہم آئے کہاں سے
سنی ہے کہانی ، فقط درمیاں سے

As we open our eyes and look at our world, we find that there are things around us about which we know nothing with any certainty. How did our Universe come about? How did this story begin? Who lived here before us? How old was this earth when the first man set foot on it? What is the purpose of those countless stars and galaxies that we see on our night sky? What happens to us when we die.? Despite advancement in our knowledge through recent scientific discoveries, we are still looking for answers to many of these basic questions. Each time we think we have unraveled a mystery, it leads us to further questions and proves yet again that what we had believed to be true, may not be necessarily so. Where is the answer then, to our questions and is there anyone who knows the answer? Who knows exactly when this story began? We experience or witness this "phenomenon", at a certain point, for a brief time and then we leave. How can we get the whole picture?

Does spirituality guide us in this quest? Is awareness of one's spirituality necessarily a religious experience? Is religion the answer? If so, which religion? Does one have to belong to an organized religious group to be considered religious.? Is religion necessary in this age of scientific advancement.? Does a belief system have a place in an advanced secular society like the one we live in today, especially the west? These are the questions that intrigue us and demand a measured answer.

I have, for long, felt the need to write in a simplified format, all that I have observed and learnt over the years, about the human experience on this planet and our collective understanding of the purpose of our existence. Pace of life in the western world as it is, none of us in our formative and schooling years has the time to study or ponder over things that are not in our syllabus. Yet that is the time when our moral and ethical being is taking shape. Unless we are introduced to our spiritual being at that early age, we lose out on a very essential aspect of our development. That aspect, in my view, is the true essence of our life.

Earth has become a global village. Our neighbors and co-workers in this "Global Village", especially in these United States are of many diverse backgrounds. Our children are being raised in this multiethnic and multicultural environment and are exposed to quite diverse and at times conflicting cultural data sets. It is necessary that we provide at least some basic information about religion to our children, to avoid creating a vacuum. Since an interfaith dialogue is a reality and a true need of our times, to participate in such a dialogue, as a start, our future generations must have some information about the religion in which they are borne. Ignoring this fact can lead to our children feeling inadequate in partaking in this dialogue, thus maintaining that awareness gap that currently exists, keeping us suspicious of our neighbors with a different belief system.

I have tried to simplify the discourse – to the extent possible by staying brief and simple, yet not too elementary or superficial. The purpose is to expose the reader to the material from various belief systems and highlight the similarities and point out any major divergence of opinion. Inquisitive readers will then follow whatever lead is of interest to them and delve into it further on their own. The message I took to heart as I put all this together is that in our make-up, we are all the same. Spirit within all of us is of the same nature and from the same source. We as humans have, but a limited capacity, to understand our creator or true nature of this universe. A huge body of knowledge is hidden from us (by design), and we should not deny its existence. If we bring back from the ocean, all the water that we can carry, we might have a lot, but it is miniscule compared to what remains in the ocean. The created universe is much larger and more profound than the man has seen or understood thus far. The realization of our limitations is the key to our opening up to the "Ultimate Truth".

These days, one is afraid of touching any subject that is somehow related to a religion or faith system. This "tabooing" of everything religious, has resulted in one unintended result – a vacuum in essential knowledge about belief systems. People are afraid to discuss their own religion in their own households, with their own families and especially the children. This simple omission, in my view, is resulting in a gap in the learning process that has far reaching consequences. Children grow up not knowing anything about any belief system, including the one they were borne in. It is especially true for those families where the parents are non-practicing and have not been able to expose their young children to their religion of birth. This makes them ill prepared to deal with their peers with religious inclinations. Without a reference point, it is hard to relate to others and be a constructive member of a multifaceted society. The need is even greater now since our exposure to people with different faith systems is increasing in today's world that truly is becoming like one big family.

Since "an idle mind is a devil's workshop", the void is filled in later life, by misinformation and becomes a fertile ground for negative propaganda. Such naïve and innocent minds are vulnerable and can be easily manipulated by the extraneous influences, be it media or the political entities, in demonizing a certain segment of society or faith system. It is impossible for them to realize that the opinion they subscribe to or endorse, may in fact, be flawed or incorrect. This phenomenon unfortunately, is not conducive to establishing a healthy and progressive society in our world.

Much that I loved spirituality all my life, I had natural hesitancy in expressing myself on this subject mindful of the fact that this is a subject that is vast as well as profound. Views and opinions on this subject differ not only between religions and faith systems but oftentimes also within the same belief system. The reader decides what explanation appeals to his or her mind and then can build a concept on or around it to satisfy the inner need. After having spent over seven and a half decades on this earth, I feel that I should share the experience I have gained over the years. Besides – my thoughts probably are as mature as they will ever get and if I don't harvest their fruit, it might start dropping off in the wasteland of senility. I have benefited from the world literature on this subject, in putting together the material for this book. Everything between these cover pages is not my own idea. A sincere effort is made to benefit from the available knowledge and present it in a simplified way so that an average reader can get a broader picture of the subject.

Being brought up and schooled in practically a single-faith environment in Pakistan and then spending most of my adult life in the melting pot (or the salad bowl, depending on your point of view) called "The United States of America", I am fortunate to have had the opportunity to experience life with a uniquely broader perspective. Add to this background the fact that as a practicing physician, I had to interact with a broad section of populace with different socioeconomic strata and religious and cultural backgrounds, in a very private and personal settings, often over significantly extended periods. Being a Hematologist-Oncologist and working in "Hospice" and end of life care settings, I witnessed a plethora of human emotions among the terminally ill patients and their loved ones. This invaluable exposure is a great teacher for one who is open to learn.

It is my strong belief that given all that I mentioned above, one must have a good understanding of different belief systems and cultures in the world. Regardless of one's starting point, one must approach this subject with an open mind. Reality might look different in the beginning, to different faith systems or groups but then it starts to converge. At a certain mature age and above a certain stratum of learning, the path to reality seems to become one and the same for all. That is why one notices a greater tolerance and more accommodation of other belief systems in those sages, mystics and saints who have attained that status and are able to reside in our commonality. Will this reality ever dawn on our day to day, religiously rigid, uncompromising clergy, is anyone's guess.

...

Abdul Rehman Abd.

A common mistake a person makes while trying
to understand his world, is his total reliance on his
INTELECT.

There are countless sights we are incapable of seeing
and countless sound frequencies that we cannot hear.

***

Chapter 1

"I"

Life on Earth is a test. My identity is the Spirit within me that is pure at birth.
If I can connect with it, nurture it and keep it pure, I pass the test.
My challenges are the corrupting nature of this world
and the corrupting desires of my physical body.
....

The Time on Earth.

Your life is only the choices you make.

The Journey of life:

...

If you can't seem to find the purpose of life,
let your life find its purpose by
living its passion.

All humans are borne, pure and clean, with the similar innate nature and instincts. The environment, upbringing and exposure to various surrounding elements shape them into various kinds of travelers through this life journey. Some of us get the direction and the message early on and find a mission for our lives but scores of others get lost in this sea of existence. Such is the model of this human experiment on Earth.

Quite simply, a child of Adam comes into this world as a physical being, for a finite time. His identity is his soul that was created eons ago in a different realm. This soul is given a vehicle to travel - his earthly body. It is the job of this soul to use the vehicle, control it well and get across this vast valley of life, to reach on the other side to its destination. But wait. It is not that simple.

Along the way, there will be temptations and distractions. Difficulty factors will be added to further challenge the traveler to see who does well. This journey is but a test. There are the elements of free will, ego and so called "logical thinking" to deal with. For the believers of the Divine religion, there is the element of "Satan" that is at play. This is the entity that is hellbent *(with Divine permission), to distract the traveler and derail him or her from the right track. Now the fun part (the life) starts.

Every traveler has the same intrinsic make up (pure soul), and the same "inwardly resources" (instinct, nature, intuitions etc.), but the external environment and influences are variable. It depends on when you appear in this world, where do you appear and what external forces and challenges are at play at that location. These same challenges will be faced by others on the same journey that are your peers or co-travelers. Your challenge is to use your resources to understand your mission and get across this testing ground making the right choices along the way.

Al-Ghazali, (Al'chemy of happiness) describes this process in a beautiful way. Paraphrased, it basically states that your physical body is the Horse given to you to ride across the valley of Life. Your soul (Spirit / Rouh) is the rider on that horse, that controls it and directs it as to where to go or not to go. Your job is to nurture both elements, body as well as your spirit or Rouh (soul) appropriately, keep them on their mission and not be swayed by the distractions that surround them in this world.

Feed your Spirit so that it is strong enough to control the horse that is your body. If your horse (body) overpowers your spirit, it will be out of control and will not be able to differentiate right from wrong. The Horse will trample into the fields and the crops of others, causing destruction, strife and chaos. It will take you away from your path, into the fields of lust, greed and worldly pleasures. You will be lost. On the other hand, if your spirit (Soul, the rider) is well fed, strong enough to control your body (horse), you will get across this valley of life unscathed and successful. The mission of life accomplished.

Now the question is, how to feed the inner spirit, strengthen it and enable it to control the body. That is where spirituality serves as the "Guidebook". It is by recognizing the spiritual part of our being that we begin this process. Be mindful of the fact that your body belongs to this world. It is comprised of the earthly elements. Its nourishment also comes from the resources that are present here on this planet. The spirit within the body, however, is from a different realm. It is from the Divine - or supernatural for those who do not believe in God. Its nourishment must also come from that realm. To nurture the soul, one must connect it to that realm to receive its sustenance.

There are ways to connect to that realm and nurture our inner spirit. Basic to this process is the act of temporarily disconnecting from our world by shutting down the input from our five senses. In practically every culture, humans have found or developed the techniques to disconnect from our five senses, weather it is Prayers, Chanting, Yoga, Meditative routines, or whirling etc. The idea is to concentrate on a point within yourself and block out all thoughts and influences from the outside world. Listen to your inner voice. Connect to that inner spirit within you. Then, depending upon your spiritual make up, sincerity and effort, you will be able to start empowering your spirit. You will cleanse your soul, like one cleans the dusty and rusty mirror. This rusty mirror, i.e., your heart that is polluted by bad deeds and corrupted by worldly desires, starts to shine and get purified. Change can be from being totally opaque to perfectly clean and reflective or several stages in between.

One grows spiritually from being rogue and devilish to being saintly and reflective of the Divine. Can anybody and everybody do it? That is a tough call. From what one learns from the religious scriptures; it seems that there always will be evil in the world. This is how the system is designed to be a perfect testing ground. There is good with bad, light with darkness and truth with falsehood. It seems that the system needs all these elements to operate as intended. Those who ponder upon the reason for their existence and choose to live up to their potential are the ones that will be successful in this test of life. Faith may be the easiest way to accomplish that.

It is better to move on with the roadmap at hand than to spend a lifetime, standing still, trying to prove or disprove the authenticity of that Roadmap.

....

Does one need a faith system or religion to be spiritual? This is a hot question of our time. With emergence of secular societies and freedom of religion and more importantly, the freedom "from" religion, the topics of Religions, need for Religions and the social impact of religiosity is getting a lot of attention. This indeed is a tough cliff to climb. That reminds me of a fable that makes a pro-faith point and is in conformity with my own personal view on this matter.

A group of people lived within an eyeshot of a tall mountain and always wondered what it would be like to be on the top of that mountain. Curiosity led to the desire and they decided to find ways to conquer that mountain. Those with the faith disappeared into some cave and were never seen again. The intellectuals and those with worldly and scientific education started their approach to this challenge by using scientific techniques and climbing tools. They started to climb ever so carefully making progress every year. After several years and scores of tragical events some of them finally reached the peak, only to find that those with faith that had disappeared in a cave, have been camped on the mountaintop comfortably for years.

Implicit in the story is the notion that one has a choice of wandering through the wilderness of this life, unguided or get a password for the mega-computer that is the spirit within you and start surfing the universe wide web in milliseconds. Students of Kabbalah can understand this example better, given the teachings of early Kabbalists and the protection of this secret "received" knowledge. This subject will be dealt with, in more detailed manner later in this book.

Sufism, in Islam teaches the path of spiritual ascension and becoming a "Friend of God" (or among the Awlia-Allah), by :-

(a) connecting to a source of "received knowledge", i.e. joining a "silsila", or line of spiritual connection, and having a spiritual guide. This shows your intention to travel this path, realizing that it is not going to be easy. This makes you "Mureed", i.e. the one with the intention.

(b) Total reliance on God for all affairs and weaning off from the worldly desires and possessions. Being true to the word "You cannot serve two masters".

(c) Being "God-Conscious" all the time and leaving all your affairs to God and accepting what comes your way as the will of God.

(d) Getting to the stage of soul purification and spiritual status when you begin to do the Divinely command deeds and have no fear of worldly consequences.

It wouldn't be out of place to narrate here, a story that illustrates the point:-

A saintly man was walking in the Bazar wearing sloppy wooden slippers, with his shabby garb wet with rain. A merchant saw him and felt that he must be cold and hungry. He invited him up in his shop and offered him some warm milk to drink. After drinking the milk, the man thanked the shopkeeper and went about his way. As he turned the corner, there was a beautiful young lady sitting on the steps of a house, alongside her man friend. Accidentally, some muddy water from the wooden slippers of this saintly man splashed on the clean clothes of this lady. Her friend got infuriated and slapped this man harshly on his face, landing him in that muddy water. The old man managed to pick himself up, looked up to the sky and murmured to himself: *"Who can understand your doings, oh God. One minute you offer me warm milk and the comfort of a warm place and the next minute you slap me on the face and throw me in the mud."*

As he walks down a block or two, a man runs up to him from behind and grabs him by his shirt, demanding an explanation. Why did you curse that woman, because she has fallen from the steps and is  critically injured? A crowd gathered around them. The man assured everyone that he did not curse that woman, nor did he have any ill will for her. It was not our fight. This must have been a fight between friends – mine and hers.

When you become so close to God that he takes you as his friend, then he is by your side all the time and you have no fear. You are under God's protection all the time and anything and everything that you do is for him and because of him. That is a

24

state of high spiritual excellence. Further details and explanations of such events or such individuals, are not in the domain of casual readers or ordinary people and are therefore better left for actual practitioners of spirituality.

"Each faculty of ours delights in that for which it was created: lust delights in accomplishing desire, anger in taking vengeance, the eye in seeing beautiful objects and the ear in hearing harmonious sounds. The highest function of the soul of man is perception of truth in this accordingly it finds its special delight".

Al-Ghazzali – The Alchemy of happiness.

Chapter 2

Truth.

The House where the Truth resides

Through prayer, meditation and introspection, connect with your inner self. That will open a window into a different realm of life, to a world beyond these horizons.

...

One always wonders about the existence of so many Religions and Belief systems in the world. They all have their own explanations about the Creator and the creation of our universe. There is yet another large group, getting larger by the day, that does not believe in any Creator or organized faith system. They have their own explanation of how we all came about. If all of us are trying to find answers to the same questions, then why is it that we have dozens of answers. All of us cannot be right, or are we? This curiosity is compounded by the fact that practically all the belief systems and sects have intellectuals and well-educated individuals in them who believe that they are right, and others are wrong. It seems that every belief system can give convincing arguments to its followers that they are right in believing what they believe.

26

How does one decide? Is it possible that all these belief systems are right if they act within the framework, they have designed for themselves and do not pass judgement on, or condemn others for their belief systems? Did the creator give us a free choice to metaphorically pick a game in life, play by its rules and let others play whatever game they choose with its own set of rules? Is it possible that if we sense a higher being as a controlling power and feel humble before him, we all are believers regardless of the sect or the creed we place ourselves in?

To use the current day computer terminology, is it possible that we are sent here with a programmed hardware (brain/instinct) and have been assigned our own group user ID's and slightly variable but group specific passwords, to surf the world wide web in search of answers to our innate questions. We may have different operating systems and will need to use software packages that are compatible to our operating system, but our goal is the same. We draw power source and the signal from the different communities we live in but all who want to use the computer have access to the same world wide web. We are all searching the truth and seem to do so sincerely.

Taking it a step further, our ultimate purpose is to get to the point when you can have access to a Universe wide web. This is the common data source for all the operating systems. When you reach that level, you no longer belong to a sect or religion. Now you are on a superhighway that encircles the "House of Truth", like a Beltway. From that Beltway, you can enter the house of truth from any angle and it will get you to that central focal point, the house where the truth resides.

Look at your Universe. None of this can be random. For such a precise and complex system to work so perfectly, there must be an organization of sorts that maintains the system from top, all the way down to the local street level. To continue with the symbolic example of the computer system, there must be a mechanism to troubleshoot at local level for this programmed hardware that we call our brain or intellect. It seems that there is such an arrangement but most of us are not aware of it and do not have to be aware of it. It works without us having to worry about its hierarchy or organizational structure. May be, there are people amongst us, most of them quite ordinary looking, that carry out the Divine task. In other words, that "Higher Power" is now getting the work done through us, without revealing itself or without having to take a material form. In other words, the Divine help comes to you through ordinary looking people or entities. You call it a coincidence and think nothing of it as to how it came about. You simply carry on with your life. In other words, your computer gets fixed by a local dealer down the street and that is all that is needed at your end. The system of "dealership" and its licensing is not a matter of your interest or concern.

Spiritualists will tell you that this system is well established, and its secret is the "received knowledge" or "given knowledge" that some amongst us possess. The Jewish word Kabbalah means exactly that – the received knowledge. This knowledge is passed down from a generation to the next and its practitioners are required to stay quiet about it and use it when and where they are told. Using the computer example again, it is like giving someone exclusive access to certain special functions or sites by a password that others don't have. Kabbalists (Jewish mystics) passed this to their special disciples and Muslim Sufi orders have this linkage that connects today's Sufi to the Masters all the way up to the time when the Prophet of Islam walked amongst his companions. Central to this system is total submission to the will of the Creator and the belief that all power belongs to Him.

Chapter 3

... Romans theorized in 4th century that the Sun circled around the Earth and that there was a God up in Heaven, who created the Earth in seven days. It was not until late 16th century that Galileo Galilei and Copernicus discovered that the Earth is round, and it circles around the Sun daily.

Knowledge ....
and the seat of Knowledge.

Essentially, all we need to know is, who we are, why we are here and what becomes of us when we die.

Knowledge is the gift for man from his Creator. This is what made "Man", the best of the creations. Angels had to bow down to Adam upon command from their Creator, because Adam had knowledge about things that angels did not have. Yet, Adam didn't have to move a finger to get that knowledge. That knowledge was given to him by his Creator, instilled into his being by ways that only the Creator knows. Knowledge is a part of a bigger package called "Nutq", the ability to express. That entails the ability to receive and perceive information from the surroundings, process it intelligently as to its nature and effects and mount a response to it by bringing appropriate organs of the body into action. Our Creator makes special mention of this faculty in man, where he talks about the creation of Man and teaching him the "Bayan", i.e. speech. (Al-Rakhman-v3)

Best of the creations that the Man is, Man must realize that with all the knowledge that he can have, he will never have more than a miniscule of a miniscule portion of the body of knowledge that is out there. Man's universe is almost negligible compared to the Universe out there. There is knowledge we can have and there is knowledge that we cannot have. Quite frankly, there is really no need for us to know about things that are not pertinent to our lives on Earth. For example, when it comes to the nature of Human Soul, the scripture tells us that we are given, but a little information about it. Our curiosity can make us conjecture but in the great scheme of things, we do not need to know.

There are three types of Knowledge that a man can have in worldly life.

1. Knowledge related to physical survival - work.
   (Ilm-e-Kasbi)

2. Inspired knowledge. Given by others
   (Ilm-e-Kashfi)

3. Given directly by the Creator.
   (Ilm-e-Ladunni)

The first kind of knowledge one gets from the books and in learning institutions. This is basically for our bodily survival and is the result of our own efforts. The seat of this knowledge is the memory bank in our brain. You can easily understand that this has a very limited timespan and warranty.

The second type of knowledge is the given knowledge from the Divine source through an intermediary. That intermediary could be one's intense worship, one's spiritual mentor or guide, or by intuition or dreams. This knowledge is contained in an entity labelled "Qalb", or heart of Man. This entity is something other than the pulsating and blood pumping heart that we have in our chest. In today's lingo, that "Mother of a computer chip" is in our chest somewhere and its potential is beyond our comprehension.

The third type of knowledge is given directly from the Divine and has no intermediary. A large portion of knowledge belongs in this category, and we cannot do anything by way of worship or any act of piety to become worthy of it or entitled to it. This is the knowledge of The Almighty and the wisdom behind its nature and distribution is beyond our intellectual capacity. Humanity at large does not and need not know about this knowledge. We simply have to acknowledge its existence and understand that the Creator has designed this universe and he is running its affairs.

There is another way of simplifying the types and classification of human knowledge. By this classification, there are two classes of knowledge. One is at your tongue and that is for the affairs of Man. The other is in your heart and this is the one that is beneficial knowledge. Here, the label of being beneficial is given to the "given" knowledge because that is the one that deals with the world of the unseen. I will not break my own rule now and go any further on the discussion of this realm of life.

Curiosity is in our nature. We like to know. We have inhabited this planet for millenniums and yet we don't have a true way to measure the content of our individual knowledge. The interesting thing is that everyone seems to feel that they know. You may be borne in New York City, live here all your life and think that you know everything about New York, yet a mayor of a European city that comes for a 2-week trip to New York and is hosted by the mayor of this city, may know more about the history, cultural heritage and treasures, museums, eco-systems, and Parks etc. of New York, more than you do. I myself have met a New Yorker, born and raised in New York City, a lady in her late 70's, who told me that she had never been to, or seen Staten Island, one of the five boroughs of New York City. By casual conversation, one would never suspect that she had little to no interest in anything other than her personal life and her job that was not far from where she lived.

Understanding of the concept of "Knowledge", is crucial to any logical discussion about life and the purpose of life in this universe. One must be familiar with the difference between being aware of something, having information about something, being knowledgeable about something and knowing all there is to know about something. Let me illustrate by a simple example to make my point.

Your ailing father buried a box full of gold and precious stones in a certain spot in the backyard of his house. You were only a year old at the time. He had taken along, his younger brother - your uncle - when he buried it and advised him that if anything happens to him, he should see to it that you get this box when you become 18 years old. He gave the key to that box to your mother and told her that he has given a box to your uncle for safekeeping till you are old enough to receive it. Your mother has been sharing this story with you. Today, on your 18th Birthday, your mother gives you the keys to the treasure, but you cannot get to the treasure unless your uncle gives you the information about the location.

Here in this example, you were aware at an early age that your father left something for you that you will get at your 18th birthday. Your mother gave you the information that it is safe somewhere with your uncle and it contains valuables from father. Your uncle had the knowledge of its location but no information about its contents or their full value. Now that you have the open box in your hand, you have full knowledge of the box, where it came from, where it was buried for how long and what it contains. You had the "Awareness" about the box, your mother had "Information", that it is with your uncle, but you had the "Given Knowledge" from your uncle that led you to the actual location of the treasure. Your worldly scientific knowledge would not have led you to this box or provided you with the key. Only "Given Knowledge" was the agent for your success here.

Remember, that given knowledge was specific for that task only. How many other such boxes are buried by how many other people, at what places, you still have no idea. Body of knowledge in the universe is huge and the knowledge we have as individuals or communities, will always be miniscule. This fact must set in before we realize that we have to be humble before our Creator. We may not be able to understand his commands or the logic behind his commands but should accept them as truth first

34

and then start to ponder about their pertinence to us and this world. Therefore, the Islamic scripture, Al-Quran declares at the outset that this is a guidance only for those who are God conscious and believe in the unseen. If you insist on seeing before believing, this guidance is beyond your reach.

We must also realize the inadequacy of our acquired worldly knowledge. Our knowledge and science are work in progress. Much that it is needed and must be sought, it will always be incomplete and imperfect. What was true just a few years ago, is no longer true since we know more now than we did just a few years ago. We have disproved many things that we accepted as facts in previous years. We must remember that our creator is the source of all knowledge, and he possesses all knowledge. We humans are given, but a miniscule portion from it because intrinsically, we are not capable of receiving all of it. In our make-up, we humans have limitations that need to be understood and acknowledged.

There are two types of knowledge. One that is on our tongue and the other that takes residence in our heart. The one in the Heart is the real beneficial knowledge. And then there is this thing called "information". It is different from factual knowledge. One may seek information through diverse sources, including intellect and logical deduction and it will be a useful worldly tool to guide you towards the house where the knowledge resides. How do you get into the house where knowledge resides? That is a totally different matter. A written word can provide information and knowledge but cannot give gnosis or wisdom. There are other sources for that treasure and the quest for that treasure is an ongoing human challenge.

There is a story related to a Sufi saint, Mavlana Jalal ud Din Rumi of Konya, Turkey. It is stated that one day this Muslim Scholar and prolific writer was surrounded by has students and piles of books and manuscripts, seated outdoors on the side of a water pond. An ordinary looking wayfarer stopped by and was being ignored by Rumi. The stranger, looking at the books asked Rumi, "what is all this"? Rumi casually replied, "this is something that you wouldn't know much about". Hearing this, the stranger threw the pile of books into the water before the students could intervene. The loss such valued treasure and the result of years of hard work was weighing heavily on everyone's mind. Just then, the stranger placed his hand in the pond and took out the books, one by one, dry as before and dusted them as he placed each of them back in its original spot. Seeing all this, Rumi asked the stranger, "what is all this"? The stranger replied, "this is something you know very little about".

This incident totally transformed Rumi's life. This stranger that was Shams Tabrez, became his spiritual master and Rumi gained a monumental stature in spiritual growth by becoming Tabrez's student. It is aptly said that "Rumi did not become 'Mevlana', until he became the disciple and the follower of Shams Tabrez. The encounter with this Sufi, Shams Tabrez, transformed Jallaluddin Rumi from a classic professor of theology into a lover of God. It seems that Shams Tabrez, targeted Rumi at a time when Rumi was ready for receiving Spiritual Training. Rumi's own assumption, regarding his scholarly knowledge had to be addressed for this transformation to take place.

"I am the Alpha and the Omega, the Beginning and the end, the First and the Last".

(Revelation 22:13 New King James Version)

"Verily, the friends of God, have no fear and they are never afraid of anything"

(Al-Qura'an)

Chapter 4

GOD..

Who -What?

راز میں رکھا ہے خود کو ذات حق نے اس لیے
جو سمجھ میں آ گیا اس کو خدا مانے گا کون

(The reason God has kept himself as a mystery, is that who
Is going to accept anyone that is easily understood, as God)?

.....

The debate about existence of God is as old as time. Those who believe in God state that God created the Universe, is running its affairs, and is all knowing and powerful. Others that don't believe in God, argue that there is no such entity as God. Our Universe somehow originated randomly with an explosion and is going through evolution. Changes that we see are random and not part of any grand design or under control of any higher being. They deny the existence of anything that cannot be scientifically proven or authenticated by our senses. Some minds do change with maturity of age and further reflection, but a significant segment of society remains true to their point of view – thus the ongoing debate.

Human faculties are incapable of understanding God. The "being" of God is such that it is incomprehensible and beyond anyone's imagination. If that being was comprehensible, it wouldn't be God or worthy of being God. Scriptures do have metaphorical description of his nature, to the extent that they introduce us to that realm where he belongs, but they remind us of

38

our inability to truly grasp the nature of that realm. He is transcendent which means that he is different from all beings and there is nothing in existence that can be compared to him. He is immanent which means all beings derive their reality from him and they have no reality of their own outside His reality. He describes himself as "Light", that is in and around everything. What answer would a deep-sea diver give to a fish if she was to knock on his face mask and ask, "where is the ocean"? You are immersed in it and it is all around you, but you are incapable of conceptualizing its actual being.

We humans are but a minute fraction of the total picture that is this universe. He designed the system in such a way that we can know him by his signs only. We are at awe at what we see as his signs and these signs then introduce his being to us at a certain level. Based on our individual readiness and spiritual maturity, we perceive him to a degree and that measure is variable during our lives. This awareness and spiritual growth can rise to higher and higher levels of enlightenment till it becomes possible for humans to acquire some extraordinary abilities. Islamic literature teaches that the Almighty says:

"I, that cannot fit into universes upon universes, can be contained into the Heart of a sincere believer".

Because of those abilities, such humans become helpers of the Divine and thus seem, in a limited way, to become an extension of his being. The tasks that they do, are not because of their own power but by the permission and the power given to them by the Divine. They cannot proclaim to have extraordinary powers, nor can they use these abilities randomly for their own benefit. Some become so immersed in this reality that they become intoxicated with the love of God and are oblivious to the world around them. The story is told of a saint of that stature, Abul-Mughith al Hosein, Ibn Mansoor Al Hallaj (Baghdad, 858-915), who was so intoxicated and imbued with the Divine that he started to proclaim out loud "Anal-Haq",(i.e. I am the Truth – the absolute reality). This led to him being punished by the authorities for proclaiming to be God, and was martyred.

Humans all through the ages have tried to explain in their own words, as to what God is. Any such description is not only incomplete but also a source of confusion for those who have no belief in God and are trying to be convinced about his being. Such descriptions are only helpful for those who start by having a belief in the unseen God, and then try to understand the nature of his being. In Islamic Tradition, there is a Prophet's saying (Hadees Qudsi), God says, "There are seventy thousand veils between you and me but there is no veil between Me and you". Faith, therefore can make us travel the journey of millenniums in a single breath.

Bible mentions God's proper name as Yahweh. This could n be considered as the Hebrew equivalent of YHVH. This name, outside of jewish literature, has also been transliterated as "Jehovah".

In Islam, God is described as "The Light of Heavens and Earth". He is one and only, was always there and will always be there. He has no beginning and no end. There is nothing like him. He sleeps nor slumbers and is all seeing all knowing. He has power over everything and there is nothing that happens in the creation that is not in his knowledge. He is most beneficent and most merciful.

Jewish Traditionalists refrain from using the actual scriptural names of God for its sanctity. During casual conversations and when not in a religious ritualistic activity, God is usually referred to as *Hashem* (literally, the Name). Jewish literature teaches that in Jewish tradition, while it is a necessity to discuss and describe God, to do so with too much zeal—to try to capture a physical representation of the divine—is considered idolatry. Any talk about God or statements about his being are limited, because of our own limitations as human beings. Any description that we make are flawed and half-truths at best. Our language is from this world and reflects the thoughts biases and limitations of humans, thus being incapable of describing the one who is transcendent of this world. Jewish thinkers have been aware of this paradox for ages, but acknowledge the need of speaking about God despite these constraints.

It is befitting to refer to the "Thirteen principles of faith", formulated by Moshe ben Maimonides, a 12th century Jewish theologian, to highlight the similarities in revealed three Abrahamic faith systems.

I Believe – (Any Maamin):

by Nissen Mangel. Mishneh (Tractate Sanhedrin 10:1)

1. I believe with complete faith that the Creator, blessed be His name, is the Creator and Guide of all the created beings, and that He alone has made, does make, and will make all things.

2. I believe with complete faith that the Creator, blessed be His name, is One and Alone; that there is no oneness in any way like Him; and that He alone is our G-d - was, is and will be.

3. I believe with complete faith that the Creator, blessed be His name, is incorporeal; that He is free from all anthropomorphic properties; and that He has no likeness at all.

4. I believe with complete faith that the Creator, blessed be His name, is the first and the last.

5. I believe with complete faith that the Creator, blessed be His name, is the only one to whom it is proper to pray, and that it is inappropriate to pray to anyone else.

6. I believe with complete faith that all the words of the Prophets are true.

7. I believe with complete faith that the prophecy of Moses our teacher, peace unto him, was true; and that he

was the father of the prophets, both of those who preceded and of those who followed him.

8. I believe with complete faith that the whole Torah which we now possess was given to Moses, our teacher, peace unto him.

9. I believe with complete faith that this Torah will not be changed, and that there will be no other Torah given by the Creator, blessed be His name.

10. I believe with complete faith that the Creator, blessed be His name, knows all the deeds and thoughts of human beings, as it is said, "It is He who fashions the hearts of them all, He who perceives all their actions." (**Psalms 33:15**).

11. I believe with complete faith that the Creator, blessed be His name, rewards those who observe His commandments, and punishes those who transgress His commandments.

12. I believe with complete faith in the coming of **Moshiach**, and although he may tarry, nevertheless, I wait every day for him to come.

13. I believe with complete faith that there will be resurrection of the dead at the time when it will be the will of the Creator, blessed be His name and exalted be His remembrance forever and ever."

Chapter 5

The Perfect Man ....

Verily we created Man in the best of design. Then we reduced him to the lowest of the low except those who believe and do good deeds

Al-Qura"n 95/4-6

A Perfect Man, in a way, is the representation of the highest point of human evolution on this planet. He has identified himself as to who he is, where he came from and where he is going. He has nurtured his soul and purified it to the point that Divine beauty is reflected in it. The Creator is in contact with him and the Perfect Man feels his presence around him all the time. No wonder he has capabilities and qualities that seem to be from "out of this world".

There is something to be said about Man, the best of Almighty's creations. Man is the only creation that truly mirrors the Divine characteristics. When a man realizes the purpose of his creation, has a strong faith and totally submits to the will of his Creator, he is on the path to becoming a perfect man. One has to elevate himself morally, ethically and intellectually to a point that the life is lived in conformity with the Divine commands and the laws of nature. The right and wrong is totally manifest to such a person. Realize that humans have a spiritual part of their being and a physical part. Man is known to be the best of the creations and the only creation that has two elements to its being. A physical part, the body, that is from earth and stays here after we die, and a spiritual part, the soul, that is from the light or the Divine. Our death does not affect our soul. When we die, our soul returns to its origin in a different realm of life. That spiritual being or the soul, is our real identity. That is what we are. The world or the universe is to serve us and we are not here to serve it. For the soul it is like starting at zero point of development, when we are borne or placed on earth. Recognizing your inner being or soul, purifying and nurturing it and taking it from 0% clean to close to or at 100% clean, is the goal of life.

To run his universe, the Creator needs someone who will play the part of being his hands and feet. He chooses from amongst his creation, those individuals who have the make-up, the strength, and the fortitude to carry out his tasks. Their hearts are inspired, and they start walking the path of cleansing their soul. Most of the time, they are helped by a Mentor or Murshid, the one who charts their course and walks with them during early and hard stages in their journey. As the process advances, they begin to detach themselves from this material world and are now running their lives subject to the will of their creator. As this process advance, their relevance to their immediate surroundings becomes hard to understand. Such are the people who have passed the test of life in this world and have become true to their mission. A stage comes when are seemingly detached from the material world around them and have become the so called "hands and feet" of the Creator. Now they are free from the worldly desires and are used by the Creator to get his work done on earth.

Put simply, the "Man", that is the image of God, starts his journey towards God. Let us say that he starts at a point when his soul is totally immersed in this material world. That I would label as 0% cleansing of the soul or total darkening of the Heart. He makes the intention and walks the path of soul cleansing by always feeling his Creator's presence around him. This awareness of the Creator protects him from going off course and now he ascends from being 0% clean to higher degrees of cleanliness. At a certain point, he sees the Divine light reflected in the mirror, i.e., his heart. The process is helped by the personal effort on the part of the individual and the special favor of the Divine. The soul, that is a part of the Divine light to begin with, ultimately is purified and clean enough and fit to be connected to its source. Then with the divine permission, the divine attributes as needed, can start manifesting from this living soul in this world.

Remember that the individual in this case does not have to be a Prophet. This potential is in every believer. Also remember that the person who attains that status does not become God or God-like. He is simply worthy of being God's Khalifa or viceregent on earth. Reflecting a glimpse of a certain Divine attribute from amongst countless Divine attributes does not qualify one for such status. For others to view upon this individual as someone they can go to and expect the answer to their prayers instead of God, would be a great mistake. They do their work the way they are told to do, by the will and power of the Creator. Their life and the example they set by their actions, are the guidance from the Creator, for the mankind. These are the people on whom, God has showered his blessings and favors' and we are told to follow their path and not the path of those that have gone astray.

Another important thing to understand in this process is that there are gradations and specificities in this journey towards the Creator. Every traveler on this path does not necessarily attain the ultimate destination of being a "Perfect Man". Everyone in this caravan is at his own level of enlightenment and success. The world or the universe is to serve us and we are not here to serve it. For the soul it is like starting at zero point of development, when we are borne or placed on earth. Recognizing your inner being or soul, purifying and nurturing it and taking it from 0% clean to close to or at 100% clean, is the goal. There is a purpose of life for everyone and God has created nothing in vain..

Man is made in the image of God and is sent on Earth as his viceregent. Now, the heart is ready to take the role of a mirror that reflects the Divine beauty. A window is now open into another world that is hidden from everyone else. Keep in mind that becoming a Perfect Man not only requires a strong conviction and hard work on the part of the individual, it needs s large measure of Divine grace and blessings.

Since we are on the topic of our Creator and running of his kingdom, let us not forget that each one of us is a child of God. God loves his creation, and he has created everyone and everything, for a purpose. In a way, we are all doing God's work in some form or fashion. Our religiosity aside, we must keep this fact in our mind that he does not need our worship or good deeds, we do. A person may be a good for nothing, immoral and of bad character in our estimation but in the eyes of his Creator he may be someone of a special higher value. Respect for every human being is the way of those who are men of God.

Chapter 6

The Scriptures.........
The Divinely revealed Books

Our Creator runs a just system and has stated that no punishment will come to a person or a community until they have been given the message and they reject it. Natural inference from this statement is that our Creator has sent a messenger to every community, with his same message.It essentially was about oneness of God, a belief in the world of the unseen and the resurrection and accountability on the day of judgement. Thousands of Messengers have been sent by our Creator although scriptures mention just few. The messengers delivered the Divine messages in the local language of the people at the time and most of those Divine messages were in languages that are no longer in use today. Those scriptures are also nowhere to be found. What we have now are the three divinely revealed books, Torah (Hebrew bible or the old Testament), Christian Bible (The New Testament) and Al-Qura'n, the Islamic scripture. I will briefly mention about these scriptures, just to give an introduction and an overview. I realize fully well that the opinions on such matters can and do differ even within each group and one has to follow one's own convictions and conscience for proper satisfaction of the self.

Torah, The Old Testament, was revealed to Moses, around late 13th century BCE., and its recipients were Israelites. It is believed that God dictated Torah to Moses on Mount Sinai, fifty days after their freedom from Egyptian slavery. It believes in one

God and one God only. It contains 613 commandments, and the Jews take the best ten of those as the "Ten Statements". Torah is the first five books of the Jewish Bible and is written in Hebrew, the oldest Jewish language. It spoke of good and bad lifestyles, had the Divine commandment, and described Saturdays as the day of worship or Sabbath. It also had prohibition about certain food from certain animals and had ordered 10% "Tithing" payment every year from surplus money. Animal sacrifices were also ordained and regarded as an act of worship.

The message was preserved on holy scrolls and these scrolls were treated with such reverence that they were not touched by hands. A device called "Yad" (hand) that looks like a hand with stretched finger, is used to touch the scroll. If somehow, during a congregational gathering, the scroll was to drop to the floor, it was a major event. To ask for forgiveness from the Creator, the whole congregation was expected to fast for forty days.

There was an oral law, alongside the written law, given to Moses, that was to be passed on from mouth to mouth, from generation to generation. Oral law has the information the believers need to interpret the written law or the ten commandments. This law was codified in the 2nd century C.E. Most of the spiritual guidance and instructions are contained in this oral law that was preserved so that it does not get corrupted by those who are unworthy to receive it. That might explain why the spiritual teaching or Kabalah", was not in written form for centuries.

The New Testament, the Bible was revealed in Greek language. It focuses more on the teachings of Jesus and the church. The one God, as in Old Testament is replaced by the idea of God as trinity, and declares that if you repent, you are automatically forgiven. It has no food inhibitions or sabbath observation on Saturday and endorses Sunday as the day of worship. It advises to give cheerfully but takes away the mandatory 10% giving, to be given every year for the needy, that was in Old Testament. The "Eye for an Eye" approach in Old Testament is replaced by "Love thy neighbor", and the approach on adultery, public giving and wordship is also softened in New Testament, as compared to the Old Testament.

Christians believe that Jesus was conceived by the Holy Spirit, was borne of a vigin mother Mary, he performed miracles, died by crucifixion as a sacrifice to achieve atonement for sin and rose from the dead. He founded the Church and enables people to be reconciled with God. Jews do not believe in the divinity of Jesus, nor do they believe that he was raised from the dead. Muslims believe Jesus to be a prophet, borne of a virgin mother and that he was raised up to heaven and shall return one day. He was never crucified but God had replaced him on the crucifix with someone that looked like him.

Christians and Jews are one in believing in the Old Testament/Hebrew Bible. The difference is that the Christians also acknowledge the New Testament and the Jews do not. There is varied interpretation that each of them makes, of the scripture, to the extent that it appears as if they are reading two different books.

Resurrection is hardly described in the Hebrew Bible, which gloriously highlights the status of Abraham as the father of a great nation. Emphasis in Hebrew Bible is on the commandments for a good life and obedience to God and little is mentioned about prior human experience or rights of the mankind. Christian Bible, on the other hand, has very little by way of the commandments for life. A comprehensive account of Human history is found in Islamic scripture, Al-Quran that gives an account of human history, stories of previous prophets, commands of life and prohibitions and the details of rewards and punishment in the afterlife.

The Al-Quran.. The Islamic scripture Al-Quran is a divinely revealed book that is full code of conduct for human life on earth. The words of God, few verses at a time, came down to Prophet Muhammad, (PBUH) in his mother tongue - "Arabic", by the Archangel Gabriel and were memorized by him. When he repeated those words to his companions, they memorized them and were written down by those who could write. This process of divine revelations continued with some regularity over a period of 23 years. By the time of departure of Prophet Muhammad from this world at the age of 63 years, he had properly sequenced the bits of revelations and had memorized the entire scripture with the ability to recite it in the sequence that exists today. It is said that Prophet Muhammad recited the Qur'an twice, in the presence of the angel Gabriel, in the month of Ramadan, of the year of the Prophet's departure from this world.

Al-Quran gives stories of prior messengers and their followers, from Adam to the final messenger Muhammad (PBUH) and attests to the Torah, the Bible and other divinely revealed books to be authentic and from the Almighty. It mentions and authenticates all the Divine messengers. It deals with and has a guidance for any issue that can arise in a believer's life. It details the orders or must do deeds (i.e., Commandments) like five daily prayers, fasting for the month of Ramadhan, an annual giving of 2.5% of your wealth that has been surplus in prior year, and once in a lifetime pilgrimage to Kaaba, the house of God built by prophet Abraham and his son Ismael, in Mecca Saudi Arabia. It also has dietary laws, family life rules, rights of parents, neighbors, and other people in general. It is a full guide for life.

The Quran is literally the word of God. God is the author of Qur'an. This book is like no other in the world Prophet Muhammad never stated that it was his word or took credit for these revelations. None of his sayings are included in this scripture. Qur'an therefore is the pure, word of God, unadulterated, in the original language of its revelation. At any given time, from the days of the Prophet, there have been countless followers of Islam who had memorized the Qur'an by heart. There is no possibility of adding or deleting even a letter in this scripture, since it will be discovered immediately by those who have the original version in their Hearts. The creator himself has taken the responsibility of protecting it from adulteration or extinction. Our creator says in the Qur'an:

"Verily we have sent this revelation and we alone are its protectors".

This is the guarantee from God that this message will always remain pure divine word, never contaminated by human alteration or editing. The sanctity attached to this book by the believers is purely for that reason. This book is like no other in the world. By all accounts, Quran is the Miracle given to Prophet Muhammad, unlike any other, given to any of the preceding Prophets. This scripture for example, has information in it, about planetary orbital movements, human embryology, that was unknown to science fourteen and a half centuries ago at the time of these revelations. At that time, Earth was believed to be flat. There are no contradictory statements in Al-Quran and the facts mentioned in Quran do not conflict with scientific discoveries of the day. A sage advice would be to believe in it and follow it, realizing that science will take its time to advance itself to catch up to the facts contained in the scripture.

For the believers, this is a "Live" book. It opens to the believer as his or her faith in it increases. It has remedy for human ills and has answers to all queries one might have in life. At the same time, it declares that it will not guide those who approach it without faith and God Consciousness. In fact, it repels those that are unworthy of it. A critic will pick up this book and will put it down after a few moments because he or she will not see its true nature. This is how this book, and its verses are protected from being uttered by those who are in-sincere, and doomed to be failures in life. Those who are blessed with the faith and believe in the unseen, read it as if it is being revealed unto them at the time. They see the inner meanings of the verses that are not so apparent to others. Each time they read these verses, they get more out of them, and they never feel that they have learnt all there was to learn. This is the beauty and the miracle of this Divine revelation called Al-Quran.

Chapter 7

.................Our life is only the choices we make.

Challenge.

......Man's challenge and his biggest Potential enemy is his own free will.

The Free Will ....

(a supreme design).

> At his very beginning, the man opted for a
> "Free will", and he is still paying for it.

The concept of free will is profound and not easy for everyone to understand. Before I venture into its elaboration and talk about its relationship to destiny or fate, let me state an example to set the stage for the discussion. This is necessary because we believe that our Creator is all powerful and nothing happens or gets done without his will. So, if everything is done because it is "His Will", then how can we punish anyone for doing wrong. He or she simply did what was our Creator's will and written in the destiny.

A man trespasses into a farmer's garden and starts to take the fruits from the trees and packs them into his bag. The farmer notices this and rushes to the trespasser and asks him to stop the theft and return the fruit to the farmer. The trespasser says that everything belongs to the Creator, and nothing happens without his will. I have taken this fruit because I was destined to do so. I have simply carried out my Creator's will, so I am innocent. In the meantime, the gardener's sons had arrived on the scene. The Gardner told his sons to tie the thief to the tree and whip him till he learns his lesson. Thief was told that this punishment was also written there in his destiny so he should not be objecting to it but see it as the Creator's will.

The wisdom behind this design of creation is best known to our Creator. Islamic literature has a perspective behind all this that makes perfect sense. However, that requires deep conviction, with willingness to accept things from the "Universe of the Unseen" or "Aalam-e-Ghaib". The elements of Earth being a testing ground for humans, Justice system of our Creator, ability of the Devil to distract and misguide us, our own choice of actions due to our free will, all these factors may be coming into play. may be the

At the risk of oversimplification, let me state that there are two elements to Destiny or Fate. First element is ordained and fixed by our Creator's design and is labelled as "Jabr", or Divine Decree. When and where we will be borne, who are parents will be, when will we die, etc. are such examples. The second element of destiny or fate is subject to variations and change. This change is still made by our creator, and he is aware that he will make this change, but a Just being that he is, he will relate it to your deeds and the choices that you make it your life. This is where your worship, service to humanity, prayers, and the impact of the Devil (shaita'n) on you, comes into play. Remember, this is law for the Aalam-e-Khalq, the affairs of the created universe. In Aalam-e-Amr, it is Kun-Fayakoun or be and it is. There is no element of time involved in that world. In Aalam-e-Khalq, Our Creator is still running the affairs and oversees any change he likes to make and reward or punish anyone or anything. This is where the free will and the choices we make, can make a difference. Let me recount the story of Moses and the childless lady here, to illustrate the point.

A married and childless lady stops prophet Moses one day as he was heading towards Mount Toor to have an audience with the Creator. She requests him to ask the Creator if there is any child written in her future. He kindly agreed to make such an enquiry for her, given the opportunity. She saw him few days later and wanted to know the answer. She was told that the Creator says that there is no child written in her destiny. Obviously, she was disappointed and quietly walked away. Some days later, standing at her door, she saw a shabbily dressed man across the street looking hungry and thirsty in the scorching heat. She offered him water and something to eat, for which he was thankful. As he was about to leave he raised his hands and started to pray for her. At this time, she asked him if he could pray for her to have a child also. Few weeks later she felt in a family way and delivered a health son later that year. Several months went bye and one day as she was walking with her son, she came across prophet Moses. She told prophet Moses that Your Creator had said that no child is written in my destiny and yet, look, I have a natural borne son. When prophet Moses mentioned this to the Creator at the next encounter, he was told to this effect. You had made an enquiry about the way things were at the time and you had gotten the answer. Later, when a servant of mine prayed for her to have a child, I answered his prayer and granted her a child. I do as I please.

Back to the free will. It is our "Free Will" that sets us apart from most of the creation. We are masters as well as victims of this free will. The fact that we are free to choose what we want to do in life exposes us to risks and challenges and shapes our lives. Angels, for example, don't have to worry. They are not given a choice as to what they can or cannot do. They have their commands that they must obey. Since they have no choice, they can do no wrong even if they wanted to, - plain and simple.

We, the humans opted for a free will. We make choices and are held accountable for what we do. This is the system we must live in. Rules are set. It is now up to us to know who we are, what choices we must make given all the options and what is the ultimate purpose of our finite life on earth. We are informed of the possible rewards and punishments that await us, based on the right or wrong choices that we make in our lives. In other words, we are informed of the danger and are given the tools to navigate our way through life by making right choices at different steps. Our life is a composite of the outcomes of various choices that we make guided by our intellect or ego and by using our free will.

Like I said before, there is a caveat to this. We have no control over who our parents are. Like they say, "You can pick your friends, but you cannot pick your relatives". That factor is important because certain traits of personality and character do have their leanings based on the genetic makeup of the individual. Weather this is ingrained in the spiritual makeup of the individual or is based on the environment and the type of role models that surround an individual during childhood years is a matter of debate. This much is clear that the phrase "Apple does not fall too far from the Tree" is a time-honored human experience. Certain personality traits and likes and dislikes do pass down from parents to children. Here in this regard, the individual does not seem to have free will. One must deal with the makeup that one inherits albeit the ensuing effect of the free will can modify and mold it into a different being with passage of time. That free will, however, does not become a practical reality for a human child until a few years later. Those initial years of life, the child is exposed to the environment of his parents or guardians. That influence is a significant factor in sowing the seeds of character traits that will shape the life in later years. One can easily flow into the pattern of life that evolves out of those character traits or make different choices when the free will comes into play in adult life.

We make our own life by the choices we make as we walk this earth. What we read, what we watch, and who we associate with, all of it shapes our character and our life. One who wants to be an eagle will have to fly with eagles. You can't expect to fly like an eagle if all you do is surround yourself with crows. Our environment affects us in ways we may not be able to comprehend. This realization is important because, to a considerable extent, the environment we choose is in our control.

Here, the free will comes into play. One avoids the "negatives and the downers" in life and tries to surround oneself by the influences that are positive and uplifting. Who has not met the kind of people who always start their conversation by telling you how miserable they feel because of their sickness, troubled relationship, or miserable weather? They will start the details of their last doctor visit and there is no stopping them. They would make you believe that anything that can ever go wrong, has gone wrong with them. It is not necessarily to gain sympathy, rather, this becomes their actual reality. They truly dwell in that feeling and by repeating it time and again it becomes their life. By holding on to such feelings, one not only loses any hope to realize one's own potential but becomes a downer for others. This world is full of such people and all of us know a few of them that live around us. The challenge is to deal with this reality and still have an environment of your own that can constantly charge you and uplift you to a life of success. That success can be in worldly gains or in achieving spiritual enlightenment. Understanding the need for both, a balance in them and finding your own mission in life by connecting with yourself, is the real challenge. Using the free will in choosing the right path in life, is the mission.

It is worth mentioning here that we are all endowed with a potential, far beyond our imagination. Most of us go through life not living up to even ten percent of our true potential. We feel content with what little we accomplish and never realize that we could have also done that, that and that. Lacking an impetus or a spark, we accept what little we have as our destiny and stop aiming for a higher objective. This is true not only in material success but in knowledge, creativity and other human endeavors that are marks of our collective progress. It is a big universe out there and it is all created to serve us and not the other way around. Many of us return from the market, happy, with our small container full of merchandise, not realizing that there was a larger container also available that was up for grabs. Potential was there but was not realized. This is where inspiration, motivation and realization of one's true potential comes into play.

The human mind is not capable of grasping the Universe. We are like a little child entering a huge library. The walls are covered to the ceilings with books in many different tongues. The child knows that someone must have written these books. It does not know who or how. It does not understand the languages in which they are written. But the child notes a definite plan in the arrangement of the books—-a mysterious order which it does not comprehend, but only dimly suspects". (Albert Einstein).

....

.... An essential part of our being is a realization or a feeling within us that we are part of a larger cosmic entity, being run by a higher power. We instinctively turn to that power, as the newborn baby deer turns to mother's milk. The science that attempts to study and explore the universe of that power is the science of Spirituality.

Chapter 8

*There are thoughts we can't think and places where we can't be -
There are sounds we can't hear and there are sights we can't
see.*

The Universe of The
Unseen: ....

*In spiritual pursuit, better outcomes result from sincerity of effort
and purity of intent.*

* * *

Humans make up, but a miniscule portion of the created
world. Looking at the size of our planet (Earth) and its relative
existence in the Galaxies that surround it, one wonders what else
is out there. The scriptures tell us that we are given but a small
portion from the body of knowledge that exists, and we have, but
a limited capacity to comprehend. In other words, smart and
intelligent that we might consider ourselves to be, we have our
limitations in receiving the full information from the source. We
must therefore come to terms with this reality. How can a frog in
a well, comprehend the vastness of the universe outside the well ?.
Stature of a man is virtually nothing compared to his world. The
senses given to man are limited but enough to help him navigate
through his world. He does, however, have the ability to tap into
bigger source of knowledge but that requires extraordinary effort
or gift. It is not in the domain of the masses.

Chapter 8

A crucial element in all the Divine religions, is the belief in "Al-Ghaib", the Unseen. One must begin with this realization that there is a lot out there that is not within the reach of our faculties. A believer is required to begin by believing in the unseen, i.e Allah, his attributes, and the forces that shape this world. Then and only then, the guidance comes for the life and the purpose of life. Denying the existence of the unseen world, does not take away its existence but it does deny you the true understanding of your own existence. We know for a fact that there are certain sound frequencies that some animals can hear but we humans can't. That does not mean that those sounds are not there.

Islamic scripture Al-Qura'n declares these Divine words at the very beginning that this book is the guidance for those who are God-conscious, believe in the unseen, establish a system of prayers and spend (in charity), from what we have provided them. One can conclude from this declaration that others who deny the existence of the unseen world will not be able to receive true guidance from this message. The message can be profound and not easily understood or verified by everyone that receives that message. One has to rely on the truthfulness of the messenger, to move forward, till the message starts to open up to you, based on your own ability to receive.

The belief in the unseen world is a whole lot more than believing in God, Angels, Jinn, resurrection and the day of judgement. One must accept one's inadequacy to comprehend this universe and realize that there is a higher power that has all the knowledge and all the power. He gives, of his knowledge, to whomsoever he decides to give and whatever measure he decides to give. His Prophets or messengers are chosen people, granted extraordinary abilities, capable of receiving knowledge of the unseen from God for guidance of humanity. These concepts are essential elements in our understanding of the overall scope of the vastness of the unseen world.

It helps if one is constantly reminded of the fact that there is nothing that is impossible with God. Just because we cannot comprehend it does not mean it is not true. If the source of information is credible, one shouldn't deny the stated fact. We have all heard the phrase "God works in mysterious ways". Well – he does. At times, our minds are steered in certain ways to do certain things that we had not planned. God uses his creation to serve his creation and things happen that seem to make little or no sense at the time. A bigger picture might appear sometime later to provide a clue to that "Divine" intervention.

We are created with certain instincts and certain capabilities and for a specific purpose in a specific environment. Although our creator has given us a vast potential, not all of us are capable of realizing even a fraction of our potential. We have an animalistic and a spiritual element to our being. Both of these entities have their own needs and functions alongside their capabilities and limitations. This has to be kept in mind in any discussion of the understanding of the "Truth" or "Divine message". Message has to be approached with an open mind and not rejected out of hand because one's common sense dictates that. In other words, one must accept that all that surrounds us is created by God and then go ahead and try to figure out as to what is created and who or what is God. Starting with the notion that I will believe in God when I see him or understand him, will not lead one to the Truth.

Story is told of a King and a Queen that were walking on the private beach of their seaside castle. They come upon an old shabbily dressed man that was building homelike structures with the sand. As they went by him, they enquired as to what he was doing. He said I am building homes in Paradise. Do you want to buy one? It is only $10.00 each. King was not amused by this but the Queen, smiled and gave $10.00 to the man. That not, the King saw in his dream that he was strolling in Paradise and say a big mansion with Queen's name at the door. He was very happy and approached the door when he was denied entry to the house by the officers that stood guard at the entrance. Just then, he woke up and recalled the events at the beach. Following evening, as he was walking on the beach, he was overjoyed to see the same old man engaged in the activity of building sand castles. The King approached him this time, with a big smile on his face and with $10.00 in his hand. The old man looked at the King and said, the price is One Trillion dollars for one house. You sold one for $10:00 to my wife yesterday. How can you raise the price so much, in one day. The old man replied, "she had bought the house based on faith but you ae buying the house after actually seeing it. You can't afford it.

"I love all religions; but I'm in love with my own".
"Mother Theresa"

Religion---

"You were born to walk with God...So why would you walk
alone?"
……... (Dr. Steve McSwain)

Regardless of what one thinks, if there are humans, religion is here to stay and there are no two ways about it. Religion is there for a purpose. It seems that it is a Manual for the book of life. Its purpose is to help us navigate through life and understand its nuances. It gives us "dos and don'ts" of daily living. Yes, life is possible without religion and without referring to this manual, but the Manual has its purpose. This Manual has had its various editions over the centuries and has many versions in circulation today, in various societies across the globe. There will always be people who defy religion in any of its forms as there will always be people who believe in their religion's exclusivity above all others. One must understand this reality and learn to accept it as such.

How does religion relate to our journey towards "The Truth"? Can Religion or a belief system guide us to a spiritual path and to the Truth? In my view, the answer is "Yes". It is another matter weather this is the only guide or there are other ways that we can connect to our spirituality. One must remember that spirituality is not a collective experience. Spiritual journey is a solo flight to the realm of the unseen. It must be nurtured individually though it can receive boosts and directions from a collective experience. Regular spirituality sessions provide the environment and the impetus necessary to grow this seed in you but each participant in that session benefits differently from zero gain to a huge thrust forward. It all depends on the effort of the traveler of this path and the sincerity of the commitment.

Previous negative experiences with organized religion may hinder the spiritual growth in initial stages because of suspicion and doubt that mixes in with the positivity of the experience. Of course, it would be marvelous if one is in sync with one's faith and finds a path within that system, towards spirituality. That is how it has been for centuries, but can that be sustained in this era of awareness and freedom of thought. Major drawback of that system is that it compartmentalizes the society into rigid religious groups and leaves no room for those that do not subscribe to that thought process.

Religion, in my view, can make the path to spirituality much easier, but must make accommodation and room for others. This can be accomplished by a broader understanding of the needs of an individual for inner peace and the need of the society for mutual understanding and respect for different faith systems. The approach taken by the followers of "Universal Spirituality" is laudable in that regard, but it downplays the role of religion or de-emphasizes the religious practices, thus missing out on a large segment of spirituality practitioners. Followers of faith system that have found the path to spirituality, seem to feel that all other paths most likely lead to nowhere. They feel that they got to where they are, by faith, and would not associate with "Faithless or Non-religious people", as a matter of practice and preservation of their own faith. Is there concern or fear justifiable? I don't think so, but things are as they are. We must pick up the story from the point we become part of it and move forward as essential ingredient for its next chapter. This quest is probably an ongoing never-ending quest. When we learn more, we may realize that we don't know and probably never will. The Truth is much larger than our capacity to comprehend. What do we do in the meantime? Be open to other points of view and not be too judgmental.

Here, I do want to say something for a segment of our population that has usually been treated harshly by most of us, The clergy in all organized religions, the Priest, the Mullah, the Rabbi and the like. These people try to practice an organized religion and preach it. This was never an easy role to play and is especially hard in modern times. At any time in the history of Man, those who defied any religious instructions far outnumbered those that tried to practice them or adhere to them. To them, the religious preacher was a bad guy and someone to shun and avoid. This defiant and sometimes rebellious majority found it convenient to ridicule these religious figures and thus found solace in ignoring their advice. It is far too easy having a nice walk in the park than to have to go to church a synagogue or a mosque etc. and listen to someone who may not have as many University degrees as you do. Having to give up certain behavior traits is difficult so why bother listening to that sermon and feel guilty. It is better to avoid it or ignore it. Then to feel right about yourself, it is convenient and natural to discredit that individual who preaches that message. The emphasis is placed on the person and not the message. A common person on the street finds it easy to listen to follow the easy route of freedom from religion than to have to follow the religious dictates. More one ridicules or badmouths the clergy, easier it is to throw away any ties to his message and feel free. The reality is that this phenomenon is common in all faith systems and is becoming ever more prevalent across the globe. No wonder, there is not a single country in the world that has its constitution based on its religion or faith system, and its inhabitants following all the laws of that religion.

Here is what I feel, is the most practical approach to the subject of religion in our lies. Try to learn as much as possible about our own identity, our physical being and the wisdom behind the creation of our universe. Know that our Universe is a perfect design that could not have happened on its own. Someone with wisdom and power created it. Most importantly, realize that our knowledge and understanding is limited. Just because we can not see the air around us does not mean that it does not exist. Just because we cannot comprehend the eternal life does not mean that it can not exist. The essence of belief is to accept all that we can verify to be true and NOT REJECT what we can not understand or verify due to our limited abilities. By this approach we lose nothing, commit no wrong and are on a safer ground. So, in a nutshell, here will be my approach:

1. My knowledge is limited compared to the total body

of knowledge. I can not deny what I can not perceive. I am certain of that.

2. The Universe is not an accident but build on a master plan. There definitely, is a Creator and sustainer of it all. There is no harm in accepting this concept and definite harm in its denial.

3. There is this selfish reason also. Accepting a valid and reasonable explanation about life and afterlife makes it easy to look forward to tomorrow and beyond. It makes one behave responsibly in life. Without the concept of afterlife and the reward and punishment, life on earth becomes animalistic and the survival of the fittest. One has nothing to look forward to, with satisfaction, on one's death bed.

4. The discord between different religions that one sees, is at lower level of understanding and is man-made. As the knowledge of the practitioner of any organized religion increases and he or she becomes closer to reality, the interfaith gap narrows till the single reality, The Truth", manifests itself as one. The Creator just gave one faith system to his creation. The truth for the entire humanity is one, as is their Creator.

- all wisdoms is to know that there is a First Being Who brings every existing thing into being. All existing things – in heaven, on earth and what is between them

– come into being only from His true existence. If it should enter one's mind that He does not exist – no other thing could have any existence. **99** ....*Mishneh Torah, Yesodei HaTorah, 1:1-2*

Belief in One God is certainly the most essential and crucial element to normative Judaism. Belief in one God is the fundamental of all fundamentals as asserted by the medieval thinker Maimonides, , at the beginning of his legal masterpiece Mishneh Torah.. He pronounced that Jews are commanded to believe in God, and this is the commandment upon which all of Judaism depends.

It is worth mentioning here that atheists have been there all along, in all societies and probably always. Likewise, literature reveals that there are, and always have been, Jewish atheists. Today there are 10,000 American Jews and 32 synagogues affiliated with Secular Humanistic Judaism, a non-theistic Jewish movement founded in 1963 by Sherwin Wine. Nonetheless, the major Jewish denominations are uncomfortable with the idea of a Judaism without God.

The Greatest mystery in the universe is "Man", and within the man's heart is hidden, the "Greatest Secret".

Human Creation ....
Islamic concept.

It is important to re-iterate that in matters that relate to the unseen world and in discussions about spirituality, one is dealing with the "given knowledge" and not the worldly or acquired knowledge. As such, these matters are verifiable only by those entities and those measures that deal with that realm of life. Our day to day logical or scientific principles do not apply to authenticate or discord these stated facts. With that in mind let us now review and recount the body of knowledge about human creation.

According to the Islamic literature, all the Spirits (Arwah) or souls of the humans that were to come to the world, were created at the same time and reside in a different realm of life that is beyond human comprehension or approach. They are destined to come to this earthly world, at their turn, to reside in their assigned human Body, that is their temporary abode. Once their life on earth is over, they return to their original station, leaving the body to rejoin the earthly matter where it came from.

After creation, all the spirits (Arwah) were assembled before God, in that world, and were asked, Am I not your Lord?

They all said, "Yes". Few of those were selected to be the messengers of God and they had a special audience with the creator. They were told of their status and were advised of their mission to establish the oneness of God on earth. They had a separate audience with the creator and were given special instructions. Abilities and "miracles" given to them were varied, based on the needs of their time and the special environment that they were to face during their messengership.

Islamic literature reveals that every community of humans received the message from the creator, from a messenger of that time. Names of only few prophets are mentioned in the scriptures but it is clearly narrated that every community had a messenger that delivered the divine message to them. God is Just and would not punish a people unless they receive the Divine message and then reject it. As the life on earth progressed to the point that the Divine message could be preserved and spread easily to the entire human race, the need for more messengers did not exist. That took place about fourteen and a half centuries ago, when the Messenger of Islam "Muhammad", peace and blessings of Allah be upon him, came as the last and final messenger. His message and his prophethood is for the entire creation and not limited to a specific nation or tribe. This is the same message that earlier messengers had delivered, the difference being that each of the earlier prophets and messengers was sent specifically to a certain nation, tribe or a community.

Angels are created to worship God and have no free will of their own. They are to follow his commands and carry out the assigned responsibilities. Man, on the other hand, is given the freedom to choose and has his own free will. This worldly life is designed in such a way that there are opposite forces that are always at play. Man has the ability and the free will to choose right from wrong. By his nature, (i.e. at birth), man has the instinctive ability to recognize truth from falsehood. His inner spiritual being needs to be kept pure and developed spiritually to ward off the "corrupting" effects of the worldly life. Demonic influences of lust, greed and mischief etc., are the counterforces that pose challenges during life. If he keeps his inner core pure, chooses correctly and adopts a righteous posture in life, he gets closer back to his source and more in sync with it. Wrong choices in life drive him closer to the negative (satanic) influences and thus move him farther away from his origin (God).

Life's challenge is to know your mission in life, recognize yourself as to who you are and why you are here. The element of free will comes into play and the diversity of choices and opinions emerge with their inevitable results. Based on their actions and the choices they make; Humans can be successful or a failure in their lives. Those who succeed get closer and closer to God to the point that they can be granted the abilities that appear almost divinely. Others who fail in realizing their true nature and mission, have a life on earth like animals or worse than that. To them, this world is everything and they want more of it. This approach to life takes them away from their mission in this world. They become so remote and oblivious to their spiritual being that they can be almost satanic. The last verse in the last chapter of the Al-Qura'an, refers to such humans as Satans among people.

"Jinn" is another creation living parallel to human on earth, that preceded our creation. Invisible to us, they are mostly deniers of God, but some are believers and labelled Muslims. Very little is detailed in the scriptures about them so whatever little information we have, is coming from Al-Qura'n and the sayings of the Prophet of Islam.

Jinns are created from smokeless fire and have preceded the creation of Adam, as have the angels. Like angels, Jinns also are invisible to humans but unlike angels, they do have free will. Those who believe in the Divine Message, are labelled believers or Muslims and others are non-believers. They will be questioned, like humans, on the day of judgement and will be assigned to heaven or hell based on their belief and actions during their lifetime. Their lifespan is a bit longer than humans and they have children like we do. Our creator knows best as to the purpose of such a creation but it is clear that they have an important role in the overall design of our existence. Similarly, we can speculate as to why our creator has chosen to keep most of this knowledge hidden from us.

God has granted Jinns, some strong powers and abilities that humans don't have. Some of the mysterious events that go on around us can probably best be understood if one knows of certain unusual abilities of Jinns. It is stated that they can take any physical shape they want, thus appearing as humans, animals, trees or anything else. They do seem to have the ability to possess or invade another being, like a human, but such act is strongly forbidden to them. Since they do have this ability, it is conceivable that some malicious and openly disobedient Jinn, might possess a human body to create mischief or make humans do evil deeds to dispel them. Not much authentic literature exists to better explain this phenomenon. Exorcism, the act of removing this Jinn from an individual, is quite popular in some cultures across the Globe. It is believed that by invoking the name God and glorifying him, the Jinns do get out of the body or mind of the possessed individual. Some western movies have dealt with the subject of exorcism and seem to have frightened the public rather than educate them on this subject.

It is important to remember that Divine scriptures do mention about the Jinns. Some of them were deployed by Prophet Solomon to build the "Solomon's Temple" in Jerusalem. We can only conjecture about their relevance to our modern-day societies, but their existence cannot be denied. They seem to be an ongoing challenge to the believers. That is the design of this world. It is no coincidence that the believers of Islam are advised to begin every task in their lives by saying the phrase "I seek protection of Allah from the cursed Satan and begin this task by invoking the name of Allah, the most beneficent and merciful". This simple proclamation can shield one from the evil designs of Satan and his agents.

"Genesis" in Islam.

All knowledge is with our creator, and he knows how and

why we were created. Review of Islamic literature reveals that all the souls of the humans that were to come to the world, were created at the same time. They were destined to come to this earthly world, in turn, to reside in their temporary abode in Human Body. Once their life on earth would be over, they are to return to their origin, leaving the earthly body to rejoin the earthly matter.

All the souls were assembled before God, in another world, and were asked, Am I not your Lord ?. They all said -Yes. Similarly, (the souls of) all the Prophets were assembled before God and God took a covenant from them of a specific nature. Names of several Prophets are mentioned in the divinely revealed books, but it is believed that there were many more prophets that came to the world for guidance of man, whose names are not mentioned.

Man is the central character of the universe and has been given the freedom to choose and has his own free will. This worldly life is designed in such a way that there are opposite forces that are always in play and the man has the ability and the free will to choose right from wrong. If he chooses correctly and adopts a righteous posture in life, he gets closer back to his source and more in sync with his source. Wrong choices in life drive him closer to the negative (satanic) influences and thus move him farther away from his origin (God). Angels are created to always obey and worship God and have no free will of their own. They are to follow his commands and carry out the assigned responsibilities. They belong to the world of the "unseen" along with some other creations like "Jinns".

Life's challenge is to know your mission in life, recognize yourself as to who you are and why you are here. This element of "self-awareness" is the key to a successful human experience on earth. The element of free will comes into play and the diversity of choices and opinions emerge with their inevitable results. Based on the choices made, Humans can be close to God to the point that they can be granted the abilities that appear almost divine, or they can be so remote and oblivious to their mission that they can be almost satanic. The last verse in the last chapter of the Al-Quran, refers to such humans as Satans among people. In fact, the Islamic scripture reveals that it is a major punishment to a human being when his creator makes him forget himself or herself as to what he or she is. On the other hand, those humans who find their purpose in life, excel in their self-awareness, and purify their soul by submission to a higher being, become "friends" of their creator and are rewarded for their success.

Chapter 11

There is a spirit or "Rouh" within us that is Divine. That spirit bears the secret to our understanding the truth and has the potential to bring us face to face with our Creator. Our Soul or "Nafs" is who we are. It is our inner being, our mind, emotions, conscience, and our personality. We connect with our Creator with the spirit and express him through our soul. Spirituality is the way to purify, nurture and empower that soul or nafs to enable it to connect with the spirit and the Divine.

Body-Nafs (soul)-Rouh   (or freud) Libido-Ego-Superego.

The Soul...

In spirituality literature, soul is oftentimes referred to as spirit and vice versa. There is a subtle difference that one must bear in mind. Human body has three parts to it – A physical body, A soul of life, and a Spirit or "Rouh". The Soul or "Nafs" is the identity of a person and an essential ingredient for life. Spirit stays with the person till the earthly death of that person and returns to its next abode in a different realm. Body disintegrates and is totally inconsequential. It is amazing to note that during sleep, the soul is free to temporarily leave the physical body and have its independent experiences. It returns to the body instantaneously upon awakening. How that relates to the dreams that we see, is an interesting enigma. This subject points to another existence in us that we know little about.

Before I go any further, I want to make it clear to the readers that the true knowledge about the nature and being of Soul and/or Rouh, is with our Creator only. We have been told that we are only given a little bit of information about it. The wisdom behind not providing us the details of this entity, is only known to our Creator. Logical that we like to be, it seems that this was for our own good because the possibility of us not understanding it and denying it. That might have doomed some of us to the state of forever being at a loss or as non-believers. In a nutshell, and at the risk of oversimplification, let me put forth the main characters of the subject. Humans have a physical being and a spiritual being. The entity labelled Soul has been described and understood by different faith groups differently. Spiritualists in each group have had their own classifications and gradations of this entity but these subtle differences in description do not point to any difference in the nature of the entity under discussion.

The Soul, as in Judaism: ....

A lot is found in Jewish literature about the soul and the subject of spirituality. Jewish literature is quite detailed in discussion of the soul and it categorizes it into diverse types. By some, every Jew is composite of two distinct souls. *Nephesh HaBehamit* and *Nefesh Elokit*. The first one, Nefesh HaBehamit, inhabits the body at its birth and is complete with an infrastructure of soul powers ranging from pleasure and will to intellect and emotions. The second one, Nefesh Elokit, is "a part of the Divine" and exists both before its descent into the body and after the ascent from the body.

Nefesh HaBehamit is there to fulfil the basic needs, passions, and desires of the body. This, in a way makes it essentially animalistic and self-centered. This soul is the cause of all negative human traits including aggression, anger, and arrogance. *Nefesh Elokit* was in existence both before its descent into the body and will be there after its ascent from the body. This soul is pure and does not need any rectification. Rather, the purpose of its descent into this world is to influence the behavior and the conduct of the animalistic nature of this material world.

Most interesting in the jewish literature, is the detail that it gives about this *Nephesh Elokit. It* states that before this soul joins the body and descends to the world, it is taken on a heavenly tour, where It sees the Garden of Eden and the abode of Hell (*Gehinom*). A warning is given to the soul that it is embarking on a journey that is perilous, full of trials and tribulations, and laced with enticements and distractions. The soul is made to take an oath that she will remain obedient to the Divine law, and stay righteous. The soul is equipped with the required spiritual sustenance for its journey and is filled with the provisions required to transform the *Nefesh HaBehamit* as it travels its portion in the world.

At birth of an individual, the *Nefesh Elokit* is juxtaposed with the *Nefesh HaBehamit* and they both express themselves within this being. Both of these souls exist throughout the lifespan, trying to gain control of the actions of the intellect. *Nefesh Elokit* returns to its source after death.

Jewish literature teaches that every action of the individual is recorded by the "Protective angel" or the "Accusing angel", during the life time. Every deed of an individual during the lifetime is reviewed and these angels come and bear witness on a person. This is so strikingly similar to Islamic teaching of two angels (Munkir and Nakeer) sitting on two shoulders, recording every deed of an individual and producing it as a testimony on the "Day of Judgement."

"If the soul requires cleansing of any misdeeds, the soul is sent to Gehinom, which is like a purification depot. It is a horrific place where excruciating punishments are given to the sinner. This Gehinom is not a physical or eternal place but rather a temporary station that is horrifying and terrible in nature.

Jewish literature teaches that most souls stay in *Gehinom* for less than eleven months. This assumes that most people are not so sinful as to deserve a twelve-month sentence that is the lot of "the wicked". Therefore, the recital of *Kaddish* for the benefit of the departed soul, meant to bring solace and comfort to the soul from torture of *Gehinom*, is done only for eleven months after death. This can be repeated for one day at *Yartzeit ,* the death anniversary. After this purification in *Gehinom*, (if needed), the soul relocates to Paradise (Garden of Eden), where it is now rewarded for the worldly good deeds.

In *Midrash, it is stated that* the soul has five names:

Name:		Station:
(1) *1.Nefesh* (soul of vitality)	-	Assiyah, the world of Actions
(2) *Ruach* (spirit),	-	World of Formation
(3) *Neshamah* (breath of life),	-	World of Creation
(4) *Chaya* (living one),	-	World of emanation
(5) *Yechidah* (singular one).	-	World of the infinite.

Kabbalah explains that these five names of the soul correspond to the level of soul in each of the worlds. The Kabbalists explain that through successive incarnations, all levels of the soul are elevated.

Those souls that have earned their place in the Garden of Eden will stay here in this heavenly abode until the time of Resurrection of the Dead. That is the time when all souls will return once again to this world and reunite with the resurrected bodies. All opinions agree to the concepts of both the World of Souls and the Resurrection as two separate existences.

Gary Zukav, in his book, "The seat of the Soul" talks about human soul as an individual being in each person (micro version) but also as a part of a larger Soul (macro version) of the Human species. He considers anything beyond that as the experience of The Master, advanced level of light that is no longer specific to humans.

It is worth mentioning here that in Islam, fate of the soul is to return to its source - the Divine. By some, it lives and retains its identity as an individual soul (Baqa-Billah) in the larger body of the Divine or is immersed into the Divine and loses its separate identity (Fana-Fillah) like a drop of water does in the ocean.

The Soul as in Christianity: ....

Surprisingly, biblical teachings are a bit different than what the common discourse is in the streets in the Christian world. Most people think that at the time of death, an invisible part of a human leaves the body and keeps on living. This, however, is not what the Bible says. In Christian literature, one finds that there is the difference between Soul and the Spirit.

The only Hebrew word traditionally translated **"soul"** (nephesh) in English language Bibles refers to a living, breathing conscious entity. "Spirit" may refer to the "inward man" (2 Cor. 4:16) that is fashioned in God's image (Gen. 1:26-27).

Please remember that the Bible was originally written mainly in Hebrew and Greek. Bible writers, while writing about the soul, used the Hebrew word *ne'phesh* or the Greek word *psy·khe'*. These two words occur well over 800 times in the Scriptures, and the *New World Translation* refers to them as "soul,". This word basically refers to people as well as animals, and the life that a person or an animal has. A further study of God's Word will show you that nowhere in the entire Bible are the terms "immortal" or "everlasting" linked with the word "soul." Instead, the Scriptures state that a soul is mortal, meaning that it dies. (Ezekiel 18:4, 20) Therefore, the Bible calls someone who has died simply a "dead soul."—Leviticus 21:11, footnote.

Let us now see how Bible uses the term "spirit." The Bible makes clear that "spirit" and "soul" refer to two different things. Bible writers used the Hebrew word *ru'ach* or the Greek word *pneu'ma* when writing about the "spirit." AlQura'n, the Islamic scripture refers to it as the Arabic word "Rooh". The Hebrew word *ru'ach* is translated not only as "spirit" but also as "force," or life-force. For example, concerning the Flood in Noah's day, God said: "I am going to bring floodwaters upon the earth to destroy from under the heavens all flesh that has the breath [*ru'ach*] of life." (**Genesis 6:17; 7:15, 22**).

Biblical scholars seem to agree that after death, "The dust [of his body] returns to the earth, just as it was, and the spirit returns to the true God who gave it." The life-force returns to where it came from—God. (**Job 34:14, 15; Psalm 36:9**) . Scholars further state that this does not mean that the life-force actually travels to heaven. Rather, it means that for someone who dies, any hope of future life rests with God. In other words, his life is in God's hands. Only by God's power can the spirit, or life-force, be given back so that a person may live again.

Bible further teaches that this is exactly what God will do for all of those resting in "the memorial tombs"! (**John 5:28, 29**) At the time of the resurrection, a new body will be given to a person sleeping in death and bring it back to life by putting the spirit, or life-force, in it. This is what the Muslim teachings are also not much different from this.

86

In summary, regardless of the minor differences and variations in interpretation, basic concept about the soul seems to be similar in all three major revealed religions.

In Qura'an,(Al-Isra, chp 17,Ayah 18), the concept is summarized as " They ask you (O' Prophet) about Rooh, (The spirit). Tell them, it is from the command of my Lord, and you are given knowledge about it, but a little. It is by design that humans are incapable of understanding fully, the entity that is "Soul". In my view, any conjecture or extrapolation on the subject beyond this basic understanding, is not only fruitless but a possible road to misguidance.

Spirituality for me is recognizing that I am connected to the energy of all creation, that I am a part of it —and it is always a part of me. Whatever label or word we use to describe "it" doesn't matter. Words are completely inadequate.
(Oprah Winfrey)

The Soul as in Islam: ....

Summation of Islamic approach to this subject is that we have (a) Body (b) Nafs or Soul and (c) Spirit or Rouh. Nafs is the one dealing with worldly and bodily desires and most influenced by Iblees (Shaita'an). Nafs has gradations from being the corrupting one (Ammara), to being the purified one (Mutmainna) and the grades (Lawwama etc.) in between. Nafs belong to the world of creation, i.e. the created universe(عالم خلق) and is subject to the rules of time and space. Rouh or the Spirit, is the Divine spark that belongs to a different realm of life. It belongs to the universe of the Divine Order or Aalam-e-Amr. (عالم امر) There is no limitation of time or space in this realm.

Islamic literature reveals that all human "Arwah" (Rouh's - Spirits) were created at the same time in a higher realm and had an audience with God. They made a covenant with God, recognizing and accepting him as their Creator. They have the innate capacity to believe in the "unseen" and to do's and don'ts of the worldly life. This means that the man has the innate ability or instinct to recognize and accept God. This instinct, however, is subject to modification or manipulation during life by extraneous influences as well as the use of the free will that a human being has been given.

When an individual is borne, and in its early stage of total innocence for several months, the spirit in this body is Pure and unblemished. It follows the instincts and is totally non-denominational in its make-up. Influences in the environment and the household where it is being raised, start to shape it as it starts to gain awareness and able to act on its own. That innate "God awareness", that is in its makeup, now is being transformed to "Conscience" and tries to influence the behavior to some degree. As the individual uses his or her faculties, makes the right choices by his or her free will and learns of the reason for his or her being, he or she is shaping an identity. A spirit that can have the knowledge about its origin and source, (gnosis) and strives to excel by doing good, has the capacity to acquire Divine attributes and ultimately become the tool of the Divine, right here on the earth. There are degrees and grades to which the individuals succeed. A soul or Nafs can be worse than a devil or saintly and pure, worthy of communicating with the Divine.

According to Islamic teaching and the scripture, that is the design of "Duniya", the life on Planet Earth. Recall that Adam was thrown out of Paradise, for disobeying God and following the incitement of Satan (the devil) in eating the forbidden fruit. This same Satan was declared by The Almighty, as condemned forever, for not following the command of God to bow down before Adam at his creation in Paradise.

"And (remember) when your Lord said to the angels: 'I am going

89

to create a human (Adam) from sounding clay of altered black smooth mud. So when I have fashioned him and breathed into him (his) soul created by Me, then you fall down prostrate to him." (Quran 38:71-72)

God honored the first human, Adam, in countless ways. Allah blew his spirit into him, He fashioned him with His own hands and He ordered the Angels to bow down before him.

And God said to the Angels: "Prostrate to Adam and they prostrated except Iblees (Satan)...." (Quran 7:11)

Upon hearing of his fate, Satan had sought and gotten the permission from God to be around descendants of Adam till the day of judgement and try to misguide them and make them deviate from the right path. That entity, "Satan" (and his kind in humans also) still exists and is the part of life on Earth. Forces of good and evil, therefore, are part of the reality of life on earth and the child of Adam is challenged to navigate through life, making the right choices, using the free will that he or she has been given.

Imam Ghazali, a Muslim theologian and spiritualist described the human soul as the "Rider", and the human body as the "Horse", that will transport the soul (rider) across the journey of life. A well fed and well guided - disciplined soul will be able to control the horse and keep him from going off course. A weak, misguided soul will be unable to control the horse and that horse will take him off course towards the places that cater to horse's needs rather than the needs of the soul. Worldly desires and pleasures will be the mission of such an individual, to the doom of his life mission. The challenge of life is to nurture the soul, make it pure and strong and let it be the mirror of the Divine.

Just for the sake of some further elaboration, let me briefly state that the Islamic literature talks of seven stages of evolution or purification of Soul (Nafs) but three major stages are described in Al-Qura'n. These are in rank from the dark to bright to brighter.

Nafs al-Ammara Bissu' (the Nafs that urges evil),

Nafs al-Lawwama (the Nafs that Blames) and

Nafs al-Mutma`inna (the Nafs at Peace).

(1) Nafs al-Ammara Bissu' (The Soul which misguides):

This Soul (Nafs al Ammara) resides in the material world of the senses and is dominated by earthly desires and passions. Not being God-conscious always, it is under the influence of evil thoughts and actions without any sense of loss or remorse. This is the lowest type of Nafs and brings punishment upon itself by making wrong choices in life. It is mostly doomed unless God changes its nature. Al-Qura'n refers to it *"The (human) soul is certainly prone to evil" (12:53).and also "And had it not been for the grace of the Almighty Allah and His Mercy on you, not one of you would ever have been pure; but Allah purifies whomever He wishes, and Allah is all Hearing, Knowing." (24:21)*

(2) Nafs al-Lawwama (the Soul that Blames):

Allah refers to this Nafs, **"And I do call to witness the Nafs that blames"** (75:2).

This Nafs is like our conscience and is aware of its mistakes and imperfections. Here, the individual is critiquing himself or herself after a wrong action and trying to feel remorse. Is this what I wanted?. What made me do this? There is hope and promise for this soul, for improvement and progression to a purer and higher stage.

(3) Nafs al-Mutma`inna (the Soul at Peace):

This state of Nafs is satisfied and tranquil as it rests alongside the ultimate Truth. It is the successful believing soul. In Al-Quran, God refers to this Nafs, thus: **"O Self, in complete rest and satisfaction!"** (89:27). Its owner is at rest and content with what awaits him after death. He or she submits to the will of the Divine and surrenders to Him contentedly, never unhappy, or complaining. There is no rejoicing at any gains nor is there any sadness on hardships. The individual is firm in the belief that all is decreed long before it happens, and such is the will of the Divine.

Gary Zukav, in his book "The Seat Of The Soul", has an interesting discussion about the Human Soul and how it differs from other souls. He states for example, that animals have a "Group Soul" for their species and do not have an individual soul. They have only one soul energy system wherein there is no individual hood. The way of the group soul is Instinctual behavior. Souls of the animals do not evolve through responsible choices as do the souls of Humans.

Zukav states that "All souls come from the Godhead and there is no single way that souls are made individually. You are a part of all that is, and in that sense, you have always been. Imagine that God is an ocean. It was always there. Now here comes someone with a cup and reaches into the ocean and fills the cup. Now this cupful of water becomes a separate individual entity but truly speaking it was always there. You become "Micro" of a "Macro", but the energy is the same. Granted, there is massive reduction of power but the power in the droplet is as full as it is in the whole. It is just as immortal, expressive and creative as its whole. Zukav further goes on to say that "As that little form grows in power, in selfhood, in its own consciousness of self, it becomes larger, and more God like. Then it becomes God".

How can we forget the story in the Islamic literature, of the one named Mansoor Al-Hallaj, a earlier centuries Sufi? A stage came in his soul purification wghen he started to feel one with the ultimate truth, the being of "The Divine". He became so intoxicated in that union that he seemingly got disconnected from the worldly realities. Famous as true believer and a sufi, with firm belief in the Creator, that he was, he still could not escape the wrath of the clergy. All this because he started to shout out loud, "An-al-Haq, I am the Truth". Given enough time to recant or modify his claims, he still insisted on this chant and the religious jurists of that day declared him a heretic and sentenced him to death.

The world is always enjoying the presence of saintly people, with purified souls, that do the work of the Creator on earth. The rule is for them to stay unknown and un-noticed. What they have in their being is only possible through the will of the Divine. On their own, they have no power. Some of them end up touching some lives and have a following that talks about them after they leave this world. Some of their unusual or miraculous actions might have been observed by some people, who start to honor their burial sites by building shrines in their honor. There is nothing wrong with that as long as one remembers that all their capabilities were by the permission and grace of the Divine and that is the deity they should address when visiting these shrines. Our Creator honors those he pleases and grants his devotees high status even after their passing on to the other world. They continue to serve his creation for centuries by becoming His tools to serve the hungry, poor or the hopeless. There is a life after death for some souls that we can not understand but must not deny. Anything and everything is possible with the Creator.

Chapter 12

Spirituality. ....

> *We are not human beings having a spiritual experience.*
> *We are spiritual beings having a human experience".*
> (Pierre Teilhard de Chardin)

Spirituality is the force that takes us to the ultimate truth. It is the pathway to the house where "The Truth" resides". It introduces us to the nature of our being and helps us recognize our

universe. It deals mostly with the "World of the unseen". Tools for spirituality come from the "Given Knowledge" and not from the knowledge acquired personally through the books. Spirituality is personal, sacred and discrete. The secrets of spiritualty will never ever be a common knowledge. These secrets are for a selected few and if and when they are manifest by them or become obvious in them, it is time for those people to go, or be isolated from others. That is the way the system seems to be designed and it is clear that it works. We may not be aware of it, may not acknowledge its existence see or deny its premise but that changes nothing. One can go through life believing only in the tangible and logically proven concepts or have a broader perspective on life with full belief in the world beyond our five senses. We as humans have that power of choice and the free will.

As believed by the adherents of revealed "Abrahamic" religions, God rules this universe indirectly through his creation. When you pray for something and God accepts your prayer, the thing you have asked for, will be delivered to you by some means that you may or may not recognize as coming from God. God's hands are his creation. It is rare that he delivers his rewards without using a vehicle or intermediary. The fresh fruit that Mary, mother of Jesus (may God's blessings be upon her), used to get while praying in seclusion, was placed there by Angels. Let me illustrate the point by narrating a story.

A saintly man left his robe, un-attended on a roadside and went to the nearby stream for washing himself in preparation for prayer. The robe could have been stolen by anyone walking bye. One of his acquaintances walked bye and recognized the robe. Realizing that this robe belonged to his friend, he stood by it, hoping that his friend will return to get his robe. Upon his return this man asked him, why did you leave your robe unattended. Did you really believe that you will find it safe when you return? The saintly man replied, "I had full trust in "The One" who sent you here and put it in your heart to stand guard for my robe till I return."

Man is indeed made in the image of God. The limits of his capabilities are beyond his own comprehension. He can excel in self-purification to the realm of the divine. For a spiritual journey, a person must transform himself or herself from being a child of Adam, to a Human being and then to a servant of God. It seems that the agents of dark forces (or the Devil) are also roaming this earth and are amongst us. The challenge is to strive to be a good natured and caring human being and elevate yourself spiritually to become a servant of God. Yes! It is possible for humans to perform acts that we attribute to the divine. These Humans do not do that by their own power but by the power and will of God. Wherever there is life, there are agents of God, doing his work. The world has never seen a day when God was not in-charge. Organized religious orders that we see today, are a natural result of human experience in this universe. We judge these orders individually based on our level of understanding but how is this seen by God, we can only guess. Knowing that he is all powerful and all wise, may be this is exactly what he designed. We have a limited view from the vantage point that we have. The picture is much broader and infinite.

Leaving my own personal convictions aside, let me ask this question of all of us: How sure are we when we say that the only way to the ultimate truth or God is through the faith system that we believe in. For example, when a priest says that the only way to God is through Christ and all those who don't take Christ as their savior, will forever burn in hell, how should we take this narrative. A Rabbi, an Imam or leader of another religion or faith system could also make a similar statement.

This pronouncement, in my view, would be true if understood in the proper temporal context. Followers of any of the Prophets during their time, could make that statement and it will be true. It would be appropriate for example, if one of the companions of Moses, when Moses was walking amongst them, to tell a person that the only way to God was through Moses. Same is true at the time of other Prophets that brought the Divine message, all the way up to the first Prophet, Adam (PBUH). Once we understand that the message from our creator is the same and once a new Prophet came with that message, it did not mean that he negated the prior message, or it was an announcement of a new religion.

By accepting the new Prophet as the true messenger of God, one was not denying the pure teachings of the prior belief systems. Muslims for example believe in all the prophets and in all the Divine scriptures given to prior messengers. Al-Qura'n, the final Divine scripture, testifies to the prior scriptures and gives the same message to humanity that was given through prior scriptures. Our creator is one and his message has been the same. One could argue that how are we sure that the person who comes, claiming to be Prophet, is really a Prophet from God and not an imposter. This would be a valid concern. The answer would come from looking at the Prophet and his personal character, his message and the consistency of his message with the message given to previous Prophets.

Not that I subscribe to this view but let me pose this question. Is it possible that we will be judged by the rules of the game we have been given to play? May be that is the deliberate design. Whether

Christians, Jews, Muslims or followers of any faith or belief system, if we practice what we believe in, with the rules of that game, then have we passed the test? This is a question that begs for an answer. I can't help but feel that the saints and the mystics may have found the answer. They seem to have come to the realization that it is all one and the same at somewhat higher level. The clouds of doubt and suspicion are only at the ground level up to the lower sky and at the fringes. Once you cross that threshold, coming from any direction, you become the traveler of the same superhighway, the "Beltway" that encircles the ultimate destination. Any road pointing inwards from this "Beltway" leads one to the house of the same ultimate truth. Seems to make perfect sense. But if it was that simple, how is it that these "enlightened" individuals have not been able to be persuasive enough to convince their followers. Is it possible that they are not supposed to? May be this effort has to be from the bottom up and on an individual basis. Is it the sincerity of effort that counts?

The wisdom behind all this may be beyond our ability to comprehend. This is the point where the Sufi Saints would say "Wama Taufiqui illa billah" i.e. and I have no ability except that, what comes from, and is granted to me, by The Almighty God. We may not understand a lot but this much we do know. The final decision and the ultimate power rests with the Almighty. He can forgive anyone regardless of his or her sins because He is the ultimate authority and power.

Spirituality as in Judaism: ....

Kabbalah:
(Jewish mysticism)

Kabbalah or Jewish mysticism, translated as "the received wisdom", has always been considered as the soul of Judaism. One can trace the practice of Kabbalah to the early days of Judaism, reinforcing the point that this knowledge has an unbroken chain from the days of Prophet Moses, (peace and blessings of God be upon him). This wisdom was passed on to the subsequent generations by the masters as the spoken word. There is ample proof to suggest that those practitioners of Kabbalah guarded this body of wisdom for fear of it getting into the undeserving hands and polluting its sanctity. For generations, this practice was kept tightly in secrecy and in few hands. By design, there was not to be a written word. Mystics of the time found secrets in practically every word of the scripture and were reported to have ecstatic visions. In Talmudic and Mishnaic times, many rabbinic teachers were known to be engaged in mystical, meditative and devotional practices.

Kabbalah is not secret but the knowledge of the secret. It is knowledge of something "that cannot be known". It is about the understanding that we do not understand. Kabbalah must be guarded because the water of this spring must remain pure. Must not lose its integrity. Teaching of Kabbalah requires a pure "Guide", without whose mentorship, the process is fraught with danger. It is a tough process. It it came easy; it is not Kabbalah.

The seeker of this knowledge must pass through many stages of self-purification. It is stated that the path to the origin of one's soul is comprised of 125 stages. One must continue to cultivate one's spiritual self to perceive the higher reality.

During biblical times, bands of Israelite mystics (labelled prophets) are reported to have been wandering in Israelite kingdoms. They were known to have mystical powers and had the capacity to reach extraordinary "visionary" state. This mysticism truly began to flourish in middle ages in the areas now known as Egypt, Spain and Germany. It is claimed that continuous revelation is also the characteristic of kabbalistic tradition. Literature reports of many kabbalists from Ibraham ibn David, Abraham Abulafia in the 13th century spain to Rabi Yitzchek Luria of Safedand Rabbi Moshe Haim Luzatto of Italy, down to Rabbi Menachem Mendel Schneersen of recent times, attest to receiving revelations from the "on High".

The most famous and influential early book on the subject of jewish mysticism "Zohar",was written around 2nd. And 3rd. Century CE, in Spain, by Rabbi Shimon Bar Yochai (Rashbi). It was kept hidden for over 900 years because it was felt that people at the time were not ready to understand or receive it. They did not need it at that time and were more likely to misunderstand it. Holy Ari, Rabbi Isaac Luria (1534-1572), finally in 16th. Century explained the fundamental of Kabbalah and opened it to everyone. Despite that, the commentaries on those works only appeared in 20th century, by the work of the great modern time Kabbahlist Rabbi Yehuda Ashag (Bal Hasulam).

The second discipline is that of prayer. Our prayers are a spiritual communion with God through means of thanksgiving, adoration, supplication, petition, and confession. The wonderful thing about prayer is that God meets us where we are. He comes alongside us to lead us into a deeper, more real relationship with Him, not motivated by guilt, but driven by His love. God slowly and graciously reveals Himself to us while we pray, and it is during those moments that we can more deeply understand and experience His love. Of course, one of the major outcomes of disciplined prayer is answered prayer. But, in all truth, that is secondary to the real purpose of prayer which is an ever-growing, unending communion with God.

Taken together, the spiritual disciplines of prayer and the Word will provide us with a rewarding program which will lead to godly living, praise, submission, service and celebration of our salvation and the God who provided it. Through these disciplines, we are enabled to obey God's command to "work out your salvation with fear and trembling, for it is God who works in you to will and to act according to his good purpose" (Philippians 2:12-13).

The word 'kabbalah' gained wide usage in the 13th century as a synonym for Jewish mysticism. Its literal meaning is 'that which has been received', which underlines the notion that mystical secrets are passed down through the generations. Continuous revelation is also a prime characteristic of the kabbalistic tradition. Many kabbalists, from Abraham Abulafia and Abraham ibn David in 13th century Spain through to Rabbi

Yitzchak Luria of Safed and Rabbi Moshe Haim Luzatto of Italy, down to **Rabbi Menachem Mendel Schneerson, who died in 1994**, attest to having received revelations from on high.

After the Jewish expulsion from Spain in 1492, the Galilee town of Safed (Tzfat in Hebrew) became a major center of kabbalah. In 1569 a mysterious young Jew from Egypt named Yitzhak Luria began teaching his kabbalistic system to a select group. Luria, who could "speak the language of birds and trees, see the future and know all the incarnations a person had been through", died two years after arriving in Safed. His disciples spread his reputation and ideas throughout the Diaspora.

The messianic upheaval of Shabtai Tzvi was inspired by Lurianic kabbalah. Shabtai Zevi and his prophet, Nathan of Gaza, based many of their concepts on Lurianic kabbalah, but also added their own insights into the cosmic drama that kabbalah describes.

The dissemination of kabbalistic ideas and spiritual techniques took a leap forward in the 18th century with the founding of the Chassidic movement, which stressed the human desire to cleave to God. In fact, early Chassidim regarded spreading kabbalah as their major task. The opponents of Chassidim, headed by Rabbi Elijah (the Gaon) of Vilna, were also kabbalists, yet were against the popularization of the mystical doctrines.

Meanwhile, Rabbi Sar Shalom Sharabi, who moved from Yemen to Jerusalem around 1740 and headed the Beit El Yeshiva for training disciples in kabbalistic prayer, helped to spread kabbalah throughout North Africa, Yemen and Iraq.

KABBALAH TODAY

Today kabbalah is more accessible to both men and women, but it remains a complex and often impenetrable field of study. It should also be stressed that many Jews live fully observant lives without ever delving into the Kabbalah and it is an optional area of study.

Since the world war II, Academia has played a significant role in the revival of kabbalah. Popularity of Kabbalah seems to be growing among Jews and non-Jews alike. It is getting popular with celebrities looking for a counter to the exaggerated materialism of their lives. People find Kabbalah offering a spiritual path that is mystical and also rooted in the Bible. This helps unite our physical action in this world with our spiritual dimensions.

Some of Kabbalah's key concepts:

• **Infinite Light** - the light that filled all of existence before the creation. God had to withdraw his infinite light in order to create an empty space for other beings to appear. This contraction is called **tzimzum,** and is real only from the point of view of creation; from God's perspective, all is still light.

• **The Ten Sefirot** - ten qualities or dimensions from which everything in the world is composed. The sefirot have many different names, but they are most commonly known as <u>Crown, Wisdom, Understanding, Love, Power, Beauty, Eternity, Splendor, Foundation and Kingdom.</u>

• **Breaking of the Vessels** - After God withdrew His infinite light, He attempted to emanate light into ten vessels; the seven lower vessels shattered, and sparks of divine light fell into fragmented reality.

• **Berur** (clarification) **and Tikkun** (rectification) - Our work as humans is to rescue the divine sparks which have fallen into darkness (berur) and also strengthen the human and cosmic vessels so they can hold the light without shattering. This is achieved through good deeds performed with awareness and also through meditation and prayer. <u>When the tikkun is complete, the messianic age will arrive.</u>

• **The Five Worlds** -

Kabbalah teaches that there are five worlds; the world of <u>physical reality</u> is proximate to the lowest world, the world of action. Above us are the worlds of <u>formation, creation, emanation, and a world called primordial man.</u>

• **Kavanot** – <u>system of kabbalistic meditations on God's names accomplished during prayers and when performing commandments</u>

• **Soul and Body** - Kabbalists believe in reincarnation, and in resurrection. The body, as well as the soul, is eventually rectified and perfected.

• **Ecstatic Kabbalah** - Most of the kabbalistic terms come from what scholars call the theosophical kabbalah. **Ecstatic kabbalah is focused more on how to reach God directly,** through meditation, prayer and other techniques. Chassidism fused both ecstatic and theosophical kabbalah.

• **Zohar** - the most influential work in the kabbalistic canon. Written as an account of the wanderings of Rabbi Shimon Bar Yochai and his disciples through 2nd century Palestine and the mystical teachers and teachings they encounter

• **Kabbalistic Magic** - By manipulating the names of God, angels and demons with amulets and spells, reality can be affected. A generic theme running through much of kabbalah is the integration,

Spirituality as in Christianity: ....

In Christianity, the means of achieving spiritual excellence is to let the word of God be your guide in life. Let the Holy Spirit lead you to "The Truth". Spiritual growth depends on how much and how well, a devout individual, a born-again believer, lets the holy spirit control his or her life. A believer is advised not be drunk by wine that leads to debauchery but to be filled with the Divine spirit Essence of the message is that "the Spirit" will lead us into the Truth.

In Christian spirituality, one makes a choice in one's daily life, to "Know and Grow" with the Lord and keep that connection clear through ongoing system of confession. It emphasizes that a sinful act damages the spirit and creates a barrier between the sinner and God. Success in this mission is achieved by the true spirit working in and through the believer and not the result of that person's own effort. A stage comes when one is fully controlled by the spirit. That believer will be an "embodiment of sound speech, a predictably consistent pure walk and all his or her decisions will be based on the commands of God". In summary, In Christian spirituality, success is achieved when a borne again believer makes a clear cut permanent choice to surrender totally to the ministry of Holy Spirit. For spiritual growth. (In Islamic term, that total submission to the Divine, is what is the definition of Islam).

Christianity has devised several pathways or disciplines to transform the practitioner into a spiritual being. A Discipline is true component of Christian life and is defined as specific training expected to produce a desired character or a special pattern of behavior. Spiritual disciplines are described as those behaviors that nurture the spiritual growth and enable one to grow to spiritual maturity. This process of spiritual growth and development begins to take place the moment a person encounters the risen Christ and comes to Him for salvation. One transforms oneself from within and the redeemed believer has experienced the total renewal of the person, acquiring change and the new identity in thought, feeling and behavior. Paul referred to it when he spoke of taking off the "old self" and putting on the new, "which is being renewed in knowledge in the image of its Creator" (Colossians 3:9-10). To avoid error in the understanding the spiritual disciplines is to stick to the scriptural advice given to all Christians to immerse ourselves in the Word of God wherein God speaks to us, and in tending to prayer, whereby we speak to Him.

By ourselves, we simply do not have the ability to overcome the resistance of the sin nature in which we reside. Similarly, we lack the power to overcome the resistance of satanic influences that are engaged in separating us from the only tool of spiritual growth, "The word of God". Paul reminded Timothy of the inherent nature of Scripture, that it is literally from the mouth of God, i.e. "God-breathed," and, as such, contains the very power of God. He also refers to the gospel as the very "power of God" (Romans 1:16) and exhorts Christians to take up "the sword of the Spirit, which is the Word of God" as our only offensive spiritual weapon against demonic forces (Ephesians 6:17). We must begin any effort at spiritual discipline with the only source of power, the Word of God.

Christianity also emphasises the need for scripture memorization. It is crucial that one must choose what one wants to place in one's mind. Bible being the word of God, why would a believer not commit the word of God to memory? Joshua 1:8 describes the necessity of memorizing the scripture, "Do not let this Book of the Law depart from your mouth; meditate on it day and night, so that you may be careful to do everything written in it. Then you will be prosperous and successful." It is because of memorization that one is able to meditate and pray more effectively.

Prayer is an important discipline in Christian spirituality. This is a constant and ongoing communion with God. Prayer can transform our lives. God slowly and graciously reveals himself to his servant during the prayer. It is through prayer that God meets us where we are. Our prayers express our love of God and our desire to improve ourselves to get closer to God.

In Christian belief system, the spiritual journey is a lifelong process. Aim is to study Bible, trust and obey God's commands and develop a love for your creator. He has chosen to make us Holy and blameless all because of his unmeasurable love for us. Advancement in spirituality is a journey. No human is perfect. Our intention to be good, along with God's love for us, makes this journey possible. Bible emphasizes that there is only one path – Christ. We must be immersed in biblical teachings, repent for our sins, turn away from sins and obey God's commands.

Spirituality as in Islam: ....

The Greatest mystery in the universe is "Man", and within the man's heart is hidden, the "Greatest Secret".

The basic concept of spirituality in Islam can be explained in simple terms and is easy to understand if one approaches it with an open mind. Spirituality itself, however, is a subject that is quite profound and requires more than just reading about it in the literature. For it to become one's knowledge base, one needs more than books. One needs a mentor, a master teacher, a practitioner of spirituality to transmit this knowledge. One must realize that not every lesson in life comes from a book. In addition, one must have at the minimum, a basic understanding of the concept of the "Unseen World".

There is a spirit or a spark within us that comes from the Divine. That spirit bears the secret to our understanding the truth and has the potential to bring us face to face with the "Ultimate Truth – our Creator". Spirituality is the path and the road map to that truth. We humans have the potential to know the ultimate truth about the creation and the creator. We have the ingredients within us that can bring us face to face with that ultimate truth "God". All that is needed is a purified, unblemished clean heart that can reflect the Divine beauty. A seeing heart that has no barriers or limitations of vision. A heart that is God conscious and feels the presence of the Divine within it always. A heart that makes the mankind worthy of being called "the best creation of God" and "made in the image of God".

We are from God and to him we all shall return. God molded a human form out of clay and breathed his spirit into it. Thus, "Adam" was created. That Adam is the first Human Being and the first Prophet of God. (Al-Baqara). God then created "Eve", from him and human race began. Children of Adam began populating the earth and to each group of humans, a Prophet was sent for guidance. The essence of that guidance was the same. Believe in one God and worship only him and no one else. Do good to God's creation. Realize that God is all knowing all seeing and most powerful. You will die one day and be answerable to

God for all your deeds in life", and will be rewarded or punished, based on your book of deeds.

All Human Souls were created simultaneously in a higher realm of existence and given the gnosis of their creator. They all responded affirmatively when they were asked *"Am I not your Lord".* (Al-Qura'an-....-)They all responded in affirmation, thereby acknowledging the existence of a creator and sustainer of life. They join their mortal physical body at their turn in this world but upon death of the individual, they return to a different realm of existence for reunification with their source. Mystics and Sufis of Islam call this worldly life as a period of separation from the beloved, a time of loss and sorrow. Our earthly life and our passage through this world make only for only a miniscule of our total existence. There was a life we lived in a different realm before we were trapped into this earthly body, and there is a Life in the realm of "Hereafter", that is long and permanent one. We will be rewarded or punished based on our conduct during this worldly life.

Surely the mankind is at a loss – except those who believe (in the unseen), do good, enjoin the truth and patience. (Al-Qura'an.----)

Similarly, some of these souls were especially chosen to be Prophets and were introduced to each other at a special assembly. They all pledged to convey the Divine message and to authenticate and support the mission of all other messengers that were to precede or follow them in this world. That life of our souls from their creation to their entry into human body, I have labelled

111

as Soul umber period. These souls were there before the beginning of time. Galaxies were borne and Earth's creation and its evolution into a habitable place became a reality. Then and only then did the creation of Adam took place and his expulsion from paradise and his placement on Earth. This surely was a punishment for Adam made from clay and his descendants but more so for his soul that belonged to a different realm of being. That soul or the spirit was now entrapped in human body and had lost all its freedom and the company of other souls and their creator. The soul is imprisoned for the lifetime of a person in his body and is yearning to get back to its source. The experience becomes less burdensome if the person connects to his or her soul, tries to nurture it by remembrance of the Creator and safeguards it from the impurities of the world. The successful humans are those who cleanse their spiritual inner beings and make them like a shining mirror that can reflect the Divine beauty in them. Once that connection is made, the human has developed to his or her full potential and the purpose of human creation is fulfilled. Man is now capable of doing the divine work and serve his creation, in the middle of everything and yet hidden from all.

That is the answer to the question of the Angels that they had asked when they were told about the creation of Adam. "Why are you creating him, that he will create chaos and shed blood while we are here for your worship and glorification". They were told, "Verily I know what you don't know". This is what Angels could not see in Adam, his inner soul that had qualities and abilities that the Angels lacked.

Spirituality as in Hinduism: ....

In Hinduism, Soul has a central role in the origin and purpose of life. Soul is believed to be eternal. They believe that the soul continues to strive to achieve perfection and keeps re-entering the flesh (Re-incarnation), to gain life experiences. This, according to Hinduism, is the way for the soul to travel from immaturity to illumination.

In Hinduism, the concept of God is that of a Supreme being who created the universe and who is describable only as "Consciousness, love and light". He is One, all pervasive and energizes the universe. Predominant concept in Hinduism is that of a God who is not only remotely residing in higher heavens but is present inside each soul, in the Heart and Consciousness, waiting for us to discover him.

The goal of Hindu Spirituality is to know this Great God in an intimate and experiential way. The Dot in the middle of the Forehead of a devout practicing Hindu is a symbolic third eye, having a mystical meaning. It seeks to experience that vision, if awakened by worship. Yoga which means hooking yourself up to that inner being within you, awakens that third eye and enables the spiritual vision of that Supreme being.

Confusion can arise when non-Hindus see a Hindu praying to different images and shapes during a worship service. Although Hindus believe in that "One God", they also have a belief that there are many "Devas" that perform various kinds of functions for that God, like executives in a large corporation. These Devas have different names according to their function, but they should not be confused as different Gods or many Gods in Hindu religion. Hinduism believes in One God, one humanity and one world. Basic belief in Hinduism is that all the religions are paths to that One Everlasting Supreme God. Hindus therefore honor all religions and believe in religious tolerance.

Once that basic concept of Hinduism is understood, it is easy to see the commonality that exists between Hindus and the rest of the world. Other concepts of the sacredness of the Cow, different imagery for God, re-incarnation of the soul etc. etc., are various concepts that have roots in the past practices and may mean different things to different people. These are concepts of belief and can best be understood as unique to that belief system, yet not a negation of Hindu Spirituality. Regardless of what is in front of a worshiping Hindu, the mind's eye sees that one God that resides within and is the objective of the seeking soul.

Hindus don't call themselves "Idol worshippers". To them, they are simply invoking the presence of great souls living in higher consciousness into stone images so that they can feel the presence of God and be blessed. No other faith system uses more symbols to represent that Ultimate Truth in preparation of that realization, than Hinduism.

Another feature in Hinduism is "Ahimsa", refraining from physically, emotionally or mentally injuring any living creature. Those who follow this principle, will not eat meat and are therefore vegetarians. Hindus don't view this practice as a strong religious commandment of "Do and Don't do" situation, but rather as a directive or a recommendation. They leave the ultimate authority to one's own conscience. It is up to the individual as to how devout or observant he or she wants to be.

(Courtesy of Gurudeva Sivaya Subramuniyaswami)

Universal Spirituality: ....

Humanity is taking a quantum leap beyond the religions of the world. Emerging from this quantum leap is a universal spirituality (USP) that removes ideological, gnostic, denominational, and sectarian borders within and across religions. Universal spirituality does not nullify the teachings of any religion, nor does it denigrate any faith or creed. The USP incorporates the morals derived from religions into shared consciousness. It respects the practices of each creed.

Churches, temples, synagogues, gurdwaras and mosques are the places of worship, tranquility, and goodness. The divine books, including Upanishads, Dhammapada, the Bible, the Qur'an, and the Granth Sahib, which animate old and new religions, constitute the heritage of humanity. The places of pilgrimage, including Benares, Jerusalem, Makkah and Black Hills, all are sacred repositories of shared reflection. Yogis, Sufis, monks, rabbis, priests, ministers and Imams, all are the guardians of spiritual traditions.

The USP does not exclude any religion, faith or creed, from the realm of truth or authenticity. Consistent with the moral evolution of the human species, the USP interfuses the human psyche with cosmic intelligence, promoting the free flow of spirituality in and beyond space and time **Goodness.**

The USP defines spirituality as goodness to oneself and to others. Dishonest, deceitful and miserly individuals cannot be spiritual no matter how much education or knowledge they accumulate. Likewise, nations and communities rife with violence, torture and enforced disappearances are tracking far away from the spiritual path. A people that occupies another people cannot be spiritual. Social systems that endorse racism, caste system or misogyny cannot be spiritual. Economic systems that promote material acquisitiveness and egotistical self-assertions may produce wealth but bring no spiritual joy for the participants. The USP establishes the principle of goodness as the bedrock of spirituality. Spirituality is not mere higher consciousness, it is not mere worship, and it is not mere remembering God. Spirituality is goodness to oneself and to others, pure and simple.

Creed Exceptionalism.

The USP repudiates creed exceptionalism. No religion is superior to any other religion. And no religion has exceptional monopoly over truth or spiritual truth. Each religion lays out a spiritual path, good and authentic for its followers. If there are sincere followers of a religion, the religion cannot be suppressed.

There is no external definition of religion. All religions are internal to the followers. Only weak spiritual traditions are intolerant of other religions. Universal spirituality allows the followers of each religion and denomination to freely practice their faith without harassment, criticism and denigration from the followers of another religion or from non-believers. The USP prohibits the burning of divine books or making fun of any prophets held in esteem by a religious community. It guides both believers and non-believers in taking the quantum leap and shunning the orbit of self-righteousness and prejudice.

Quiet and
Personal Spirituality: ....

Universal spirituality prohibits proselytization from one religion to another, from disbelief to belief, or from belief to disbelief. Each human being is entitled to quiet and personal spirituality without a knock at the door from state officials, intolerant neighbors or wandering proselytizers.

Because universal spirituality rejects creed exceptionalism, it also rejects the principle of proselytization. The institution of proselytization emanates from creed exceptionalism, with the belief that the proselytizer practices a more truthful creed. Conversion from one faith to another is a personal choice, freely available under universal spirituality. However, criminalization of voluntary conversion is an abomination; and forced conversion is an ugly contravention of universal spirituality. Even artful proselytization obtained by offering material benefits is offensive to universal spirituality. The very notion of proselytization and "saving" presupposes that the creed of the person to be saved is erratic or inferior.

Chapter 13

Spiritual journey:
& the New Agers

Spiritual journey is a phrase used by many different religions to mean the natural progression of a person as they grow in understanding of God, the world, and themselves. It is an intentional lifestyle of growing deeper in knowledge and wisdom. But what is meant by a spiritual journey towards God, is vastly different from a journey toward some kind of "spirituality" that does not include, and is not based upon, the Person and work of a deity.

Spiritual Journey towards the creator as undertaken by people of Islamic faith is simple as it is profound. Feel the presence of your creator all around you as the fish feels the ocean water. Every act done in a righteous way, in accordance with the Divine law, becomes an act of worship for the believer. Actual methodology used for a fast and targeted spiritual journey by Muslims is described in the chapter on Sufism, elsewhere in this book.

In Christian teachings, the belief is the central theme and without that as the guide, any spiritual aspirations are meaningless. A spiritual journey filled with empty chanting will only lead to an empty heart. A journey filled with studying the Bible, obedience to what it says, and trusting God is a lifelong adventure that will bring true understanding of the world and a deep love for its Creator.

There are several differences between the Christian spiritual journey and the New Age version. New Agers say to chant mantras for several hours a day. The Bible says to have daily conversations with God through prayer (1 Thessalonians 5:17). New Agers believe that people can choose their own path in their journey and that all paths lead to the same destination. The Bible says that there is only one path—Christ (John 14:6). New Agers believe a spiritual journey will result in harmony with the universe. The Bible teaches that the universe is at war (Ephesians 6:12) and part of the journey is fighting for other souls and our own walk (1 Timothy 6:12).

Another difference is that the Bible talks about a spiritual journey and the steps through it. A Christian starts as a child (1 Corinthians 13:11), still seeing the world through naïve eyes, still influenced by the flesh and in need of basic education about God and their position with God (1 Corinthians 3:1-2; 1 Peter 2:2). And they are given work in the church appropriate to their position as young in the faith (1 Timothy 3:6). As Christians grows in understanding about God and the world, they learn more about how to act and how to relate to the world (Titus 2:5-8). A person further along in their spiritual journey becomes an example to the younger (Titus 2:3-4) and, sometimes, a leader in the church (1 Timothy 3).

At the heart of the spiritual journey is the understanding that it is a journey. None of us is perfect. Once we become Christ-followers, we are not expected to achieve instant spiritual maturity. Rather, the Christian life is a process involving both our attention (2 Corinthians 7:1) and God's work in us (Philippians 1:6). And it has more to do with opportunity and intentionality than with age (1 Timothy 4:12).

Spiritual blessings:

Ephesians 1:3 says that we have been blessed with all spiritual blessings in Christ. What are these spiritual blessings, and what do they do for us? Contrary to some beliefs, they are not some mysterious power or cosmic connection reserved for a select few. They are the key benefits of a relationship with God through Jesus Christ.

Memorization:

Scripture memorization is also essential. In Islam, memorization of the scripture is the tradition since the beginning and at any time there are thousands upon thousands of Muslims who have memorized the entire Qura'n and recie it regularly from memory. This is believed to be the miracle of that Divine book that it has been made easy to memorize. In most Islamic countries, a young child may choose to go to Qura'n memorization madrassah at age 4 yrs or so and in a year or so might memorize the entire book (114 chapters and 6236 verses) even if he or she does not know the Arabic language. As we read this, there are Quran memorizers in every country and city across the globe.

In Christian faith, Catholicism places relatively more emphasis on spiritual journey. Christians feel that they always have the freedom to choose what they place in their minds. WFor that rreason, memorization is vital. If we truly believe that the Bible is the Word of God, how can we not memorize it? Memorization enables us to keep it constantly in the forefront of our minds, and that makes it possible to react to all life circumstances according to its precepts. One of the most powerful passages of Scripture regarding the necessity of memorization is found in Joshua 1:8: "Do not let this Book of the Law depart from your mouth; meditate on it day and night, so that you may be careful to do everything written in it. Then you will be prosperous and successful." It is through the discipline of memorization that we are enabled to pray more effectively and to meditate. This in turn enables us to "be prosperous and successful" as God defines "success" for us. When we are walking in His ways and in His will, we are imbued with a new Spirit-filled inner being, one with a heart like God's.

Prayer:

In Islam, prayer is most organized and established as an institution. It is one of the five pillars of Islam. Every adult Muslim is obligated to pray five times daily as a minimum. Those who are more into worship, will pray at additional  recommended times as an optional act to gain nearness to God. First prayer is at dawn, before the sunrise. The second or the mid-day prayer is few minutes past the mid-day, when the sun starts to decline after high noon. Other timings are around two ours before sunset, right after sunset and the last prayer is around an hour and a half after sunset. Of course, the timings vary according to the season and the location on the globe.

Mostly followed optional times to pray, besides the five daily prayers, are the night (Tahajjud) prayer offered after sleeping for a short time, Early morning (Ashraq) prayer offered after the sun has been out for an hour or more, and Awwabein prayer offered, right after Maghrib or sunset prayer. Special prayer of Taraweeh is offered during the nights of the month of Ramadhan, after the last prayer of the day, before bedtime.

There are special lenience's given for traveler's but praying five times is a must, even during sickness or disability. One must pray with signs only when bedridden and disabled but having this audience with the creator, at least five times a day is a must and those who miss it, will be questioned at the day of judgement.

In Judaism, Adult Jews pray three times a day, morning, afternoon and evening. Saturday is the day of rest or Sabbath for people of jewish faith. The night preceded the day and the sabbath begins after sundown Frida. Families light candles, partake in bread, salt and wine and make blessings. Saturday morning is the sabbath service in synagogue and is the most important service of the week. It features a reading from the Torah and the prayers contain an additional section called mussaf. Additional prayers, dietary rituals and other token item at the home entrance etc. are observed to mark the sabbath till sundown on Saturday.

In Christianity there is no requirement of a daily prayer. Sunday is the Christian day of rest and most Christian's go to church Sunday morning, for a mass. Holy communion or Eucharist is the central ceremony in Christian church life. Congregants line up to receive a sip of wine and a wafer of bread. Hymns are sung and congregants hear the reading of the Bible.

Besides the above organized religious events, all three faith systems believe in praying one to one with God and seeking his blessings and mercy. They invoke the deity at certain times in their daily routine or life and believe that he listens to and answers their prayers.

Albert Einstein Quotes on Spirituality:-

1. Science without religion is lame. Religion without science is blind.

2. Every one who is seriously involved in the pursuit of science becomes convinced that a spirit is manifest in the laws of the Universe-a spirit vastly superior to that of man, and one in the face of which we with our modest powers must feel humble.

3. The man who regards his own life and that of his fellow creatures as meaningless is not merely unfortunate but almost disqualified for life.

4. Peace cannot be kept by force. It can only be achieved by understanding.

5. Only a life lived for others is a life worth while.

6. The human mind is not capable of grasping the Universe. We are like a little child entering a huge library. The walls are covered to the ceilings with books in many different tongues. The child knows that someone must have written these books. It does not know who or how. It does not understand the languages in which they are written. But the child notes a definite plan in the arrangement of the books——a mysterious order which it does not comprehend, but only dimly suspects.

7. The finest emotion of which we are capable is the mystic emotion. Herein lies the germ of all art and all true science. Anyone to whom this feeling is alien, who is no longer capable of wonderment and lives in a state of fear is a dead man. To know that what is impenetrable for us really exists and manifests itself as the highest wisdom and the most radiant beauty, whose gross forms alone are intelligible to

our poor faculties - this knowledge, this feeling ... that is the core of the true religious sentiment. In this sense, and in this sense alone, I rank myself among profoundly religious men.

8. The real problem is in the hearts and minds of men. It is easier to denature plutonium than to denature the evil spirit of man.

■■■■■■■■■■■■■■■■■■■■■■

Mevlana Jalal ud Din Rumi, Balkhi 's poetic work has been the guiding light for spiritualists and Sufi's. His Masnavi-e-Maanavi is highly regarded in Islamic literature and has been given the honor of being called "Al-Quran in the Persian language".

مثنوی ء معنوی ء مولوی ... ہست قرآں در زبان پہلوی

... A pure soul needs a pure body to dwell in.
If one feeds one's body with ill-gotten resources, tramples
over other people's rights to hoard for oneself
and consumes what is clearly forbidden,
then it is impossible to think of or talk of
soul purification.

Soul Purification.

The soul is our connection to the divine. Purer the soul, closer we are to the creator. In essence, a person who has kept his or her soul pure, or has purified his or her soul, has achieved success in life.

Being aware of your spiritual being (soul), preventing its corruption by the love for the material world and cleansing it on an ongoing basis is the key to the success in life. Spirituality deals with the awareness and the knowledge of this dimension of human life and the methods that people of faith use to purify their soul.

Key factor in this soul purification process is always the awareness of the presence of the Divine in you and around you. Once this fact becomes internalized into one's being, and becomes a firm conviction, the journey becomes easy. Minimally, the person should be a good human being, staying away from the sins and evil deeds and observant of the obligations towards the Almighty and the rights of the people, i.e. Haqooq ullah and Haqooq ul ibad. His earning should be of permissible means and and his focus of life should be the pleasure of the Creator and not a luxurious life on earth without regard to the life after death. This is the start, from which the process of soul purification begins. The journey will be towards being a "Perfect Man", realizing that there are degrees to which one can accomplish this goal. The soul is pure as it enters the fetus's body in mother's womb. It has tendency to get corrupted by the worldly elements in early life after birth and needs to be tended to. The degree of corruption or darkening of the soul is dependent on the practices of the parents and other family members that encounter the child in early life. Those who are oblivious to the existence of the Creator and are totally immersed in worldly life, get so disconnected from their soul that they lose all connections to it. Their life becomes totally centered towards success in this life, regardless of the appropriateness or morality of the means used to achieve that goal. Those who forget their Creator and ignore the needs of their soul, end up living an empty life without satisfaction or happiness. Material success can bring comfort or luxury tpo a degree but not happiness. Nature punishes such individuals by making them forget themselves by making them oblivious to the true purpose of life. They make their physical body and their worldly life as their priority and let their souls darken in decay. They lose the realization that without nurturing their soul or tending to its needs, they will be the losers in the game of life.

Purpose of life for humans is to be his viceregents on Earth and for that it is necessary to purify your soul. When it is free of rust and corruption, it reflects the light from the Creator and connects the individual to him. Those who have purified their hearts, become agents of God and do his work in serving his creation. Some get to the level of "Perfect Man" or "Insan-e-Kaamil". Nothing is beyond their reach then, of course, by the permission and the power of their Creator. One must remember that our Creator is all powerful, all knowing today as he always was and his close and worthy pious servants are present today also as they always were. They never disclose their status or true identity though some may be people we interact with and meet. They themselves never claim to have any unusual abilities.

Methods of self-purification.

(Collective/Individual).

All major religions have acts of devotion or worship that help connect them to their Creator. An individual himself or herself also can make a sincere intention and in solitude, try disconnecting from this world temporarily to connect to the Divine. With sincerity, conviction, and faith, one can feel his presence in the heart and communicate. Realize that even if you do not have the status or the ability to communicate with him, He is all powerful and He can connect with you. It is a matter of strong belief and conviction that the Creator listens to every supplicant and answers the call. Following are some of the known practices that are used for seeking nearness to the Creator and communicating with him. This is just a pointer to the practices and is by no means, all-inclusive.

Scripture recital:- The Divinely revealed books are word of God and have the impact in their recital. As a faith person reads the "word of God", it has an impact on his heart due to the reverence and the purity attached to that word. It generates certain biochemical changes in the body, based on the firmness of the belief of the listener and the listener's internalization of the Divine word. Reciting the scripture is an effective way of keeping an active  connection with the Divine and being reminded of the do's and don'ts of life. A certain tranquility and peace descends to the heart of the reader or listener and that is healthy and cleansing for soul.

Granted most of the scriptures (other than Al-Quran) do not have the original word and are not in their original language, even then the spirit of the message and the manner of discourse is such that it is not only impactful but believable and authoritative. In case of Al-quran, it is the original unaltered word of God and once one reads it, it seems as if it is being revealed on that person. Imagine, if you were a poet and you wrote a verse of poetry in English. When someone recites that verse in English in a gathering in your presence, how wonderful will you feel. Now imagine someone reading the translation of your verse in Spanish. He or she might convey the message, but you will have difficulty relating to those words and you might feel alien to that discourse.

Rosary. The beads on a string, used by the faithful to glorify the Creator, is an age-old tradition of the people of the book. Other cultures also use these rosaries at times for anxiety relief and for social reasons. Some call them worry beads. In Catholicism and in Islam, there are defined methods and defined verses, prayers or supplications that are recited in certain numbers and certain sequences and the rosary is used as an aid for the count. In civilization past, a lot of significance was attached to numbers. Numerology and astronomy were very popular, and it was felt that the time of the day, certain dates in the lunar calendar and certain numbers from one to a hundred, had impact on one's actions and supplication. For example, in Catholicism, certain prayers in a certain sequence and number, are to be recited

with the help of Rosary, for optimal effect. Similarly, in Islamic faith, after every obligatory prayer it is recommended that one glorify the Creator by saying SuhanAllah 33 times, Alhamdulillah 33 times and Allah-o-Akbar 34 times. This was the routine of the daughter of the Prophet of Islam, the final messenger of God. It is customary for Muslims to carry the Rosary with 33 beads and one King. There is a partition bead of a different shape or size after 11 beads for facilitation of variability in this worship. Larger rosaries are used for specified functions that may have a hundred or a thousand beads.

When Muslims seek the nearness of God through such worship and soul cleansing practices, various verses from the scripture or specified supplications are used depending on the instructions of the traditional spiritualists and their Sufi order. Most people carry these rosaries with them, some around the wrists, and keep remembering God' names silently as they are seated, sitting in company of people or relaxing at home. Every breath and every heartbeat become an act of worship. As one advances in awareness of the Divine, these beads themselves become the companions in the recital and the remembrance of the Creator becomes a continuous activity of the believer. The whole purpose is to be so God conscious that you do nothing that displeases him, because you are in his company and he is watching you and watching over you all the time. Any irregular thought comes to mind, is immediately confronted and blocked by this state of God-consciousness. Rosary becomes a visible reminder of staying in that state.

Meditation:- This is another way, used both by believers and non-

believers, to connect with one's inner self or a higher authority that controls our universe. Basic intention is the same as is with scripture readers or Rosary practitioners. This practice has been in use for all times and

seems to be in the make or the nature of humans. Yoga practices and various meditative exercises are geared towards the same purpose. For believers like Muslims, five daily prayers are giving the same kind of tranquility and peace that the yoga practitioner seeks. Additional yoga or meditative practices can build on this benefit and are not discouraged in any faith. If one is an agnostic or atheist, this exercise does provide an experience to the practitioner, of connecting to a higher realm of life. The effects on the body and mind are the same, providing relaxation, tranquility and a sense of serenity and peace. What part do the hormones released during such practices play, and how the tension, both physical and mental, is relieved because of that, is a bonus that is there for everyone, weather the person is a believer or a non-believer. Modern societies are adopting such Yoga type meditative practices at workplace for their employees as a secular and interfaith approach for wellness preservation of physical and mental health. In Hinduism, yoga and other meditative practices are a major part of worship. It is interesting that Yoga practitioners from India found a welcome crowd in the west as followers of their custom and trade. Attraction to yoga is much more than mere novelty or curiosity. It provides a great escape from the tension and the materialistic rat race of the western societies.

DHIKR AND SAMA'

Dhikr and Sama' are purely Islamic activities, used by the travellers on the Sufi or soul purification path. The driving principle behind these activities is to glorify the Creator and try to immerse oneself in all thoughts Divine. Starts with the notion of feeling the presence of the Creator around you like a fish find the sea water all around it. That state of God Consciousness is the main force that helps one disconnect from this world temporarily and with closed eyes, looks to the heart within our body. The five bodily senses are blocked to connect to the thoughts of the Divine.

Dhikr involves the rhythmic repetition of a phrase, usually from the Quran, in which one of the attributive names of God appears. Breath control and body movements aree also used as techniques to aid in achieving concentration and control over senses and imagination. The rosary with 99 or 33 beads was used since the 8th century as an aid to count the many repetitions. It seems that this rosary use found its way into Christian Churches from Sufism during the Crusades. This concentrated meditation can lead to a mystical trance and enlightenment which transforms man's whole being.

Sama' or qawwali as it is now called, was first developed in the mid 9th century in Baghdad. It is another communal ritual practice, defined as a concert of music, poetry recital and singing, which leads the participants to a mystical experience where they seem to hear the music of the heavenly spheres and the experience of a higher level of God Consciousness. It attunes the heart to communion with God and attempts to remove all veils hiding God from man's inner vision. Words of glorification of God and the praises of the final messenger of God are repeated to put everyone in a state of devotion and total absorption into the Divine love.

Sama played a major part in spreading Islam in South Asia, where music was a big attraction for people. Sufi saints used the mystical poetry as a vehicle to convey the Islamic message and enveloped it in the sanctified qawwali music to draw the crowds. Gradually, the tradition took roots and both the type of poetry and the genre of qawwali music became a recognized entity. Although music is discouraged in Islam, Sama music gained acceptance probably because of its poetic accompaniment and the tradition took root. Professional singers make it a point to recite some of the original Sama poetry from those times to keep connected to its roots as well as its authenticity.

Chapter 15

Seek and expect,

The Divine Mercy....................

We are told in the scriptures about the fallible nature of Man. After all, it was an act of disobedience, eating the fruit of the forbidden tree, that got him in trouble and was expelled from Paradise. We, the children of Adam, are prone to making mistakes and this seems to be our trait. Going off track at times, seems to be in our nature. Add to that the element of "Free Will" and the declared intention of the Satan to derail mankind from the right path. Angels don't have these two problems, so they don't have to worry about going off track. We can do good deeds all our lives and yet not make the grade for various reasons. Irony is that sometimes one can be so sure about oneself and yet may have lost his or her good deeds due to some factor that was pre-requisite for acceptance of these good deeds. For these reasons, we are advised to always ask for and count on the Mercy of our creator and not be depending solely on our cache of good deeds. More one gets closer to the Creator by acts of worship and good deeds, more one realizes the need for seeking his mercy. Even his most chosen people, the Messengers / Prophets felt the need to continuously ask for forgiveness.

We will be judged by our Creator for our actions during this life, mostly in two areas of our responsibilities. We must be mindful of the rights of our Creator over us and the rights of people (creation) over us. We are told time and again in the scriptures that our Creator is most forgiving and most merciful. That is so, no doubt about it, but when it comes to us being neglectful of the rights of others over us, our creator expects us to seek that forgiveness from those that you have been unfair to. He might forgive our violating his commands, but he stays neutral when it comes to our being cruel or unjust to others. Scriptures tell us that unless those people that we have committed crimes against, forgive us, we will not be able to avail of the Divine mercy. So, violating other people's rights and being cruel or unjust to others is far more serious a matter than most of us realize. It is important that we develop a habit of forgiving those who transgress against un during our lives and seek forgiveness from others in our lifetime. Not only this is necessary for our success in afterlife, but it is also a great source of comfort for others and peace within ourselves.

Another factor to remember is the intention with which we do a certain good deed. If we were careful and very punctual in discharging our responsibilities to the Divine but did so to show to the world and be considered very pious, then we will not be rewarded for those actions in the life hereafter. We will be told that since you wanted honor and glory in your lifetime for your pious acts, you were given that honor in the world. Yes, you have already been rewarded and there is nothing for you here.

Literature also tells us that if you are persecuted in a community because of your commitment to the Divine and your religious belief and practices, you must migrate out of that community rather than abandon your belief. Reward for such an act is that all your previous sins will be forgiven, and you start with a new slate like a newborn baby. That is how important is the intention of your deeds.

Final point I want to make in this regard is that despite our best efforts, we are liable to make mistakes and commit sin. We must assume that this is the case. Our true salvation is not in the rewards we might get for our good deeds in life but in the mercy of our creator. We may have committed only one sin or a trillion sins, his mercy far exceeds any number of misdeeds we have in our record of deeds. He has promised that if we approach him with sincerity, he will forgive all sins. Our trust therefore, should be in his mercy and not in the package of our so called good deeds. We must make it a habit to seek his forgiveness every chance we get.

Chapter 16

Sufism: ....

Sufi tradition of Islamic mystic spirituality is most talked about form of spirituality in the world today. It is based on the teachings and traditions of Sufi masters like Rumi, Ghazali and Hafiz, among others. Considered as the inner mystic dimension of Islam, Sufism aims to lead one from simple acts of worship to a higher state of gnosis, where the worshiper ultimately seems to become face to face and ultimately one with the Divine. Sufi Masters take their students, the seekers of the path -(Saaliks), to higher levels of enlightenment by not only showing the way but imparting some "Given Knowledge". Based on their capacity to receive, the students ascend this ladder of spiritual enlightenment.

Sufism or taṣawwuf is defined by its practitioners as the

inner, mystical dimension of Islam. A practitioner of this tradition is generally known as a Sūfī. Sufis believe they are practicing a higher level of Islam as illustrated by this saying of the Prophet of Islam.

"Worship Allah as if you are seeing Him, and if you are unable to do that, then Know, realize (and feel) that he is seeing you".

Sufis consider themselves as the followers of this pure original form of Islam. They are strong proponents of tolerance, peace and against all forms of violence. The Sufi have paid the price for this practice and have suffered severe persecution by some Muslim sects like Wahhabis and the Salafists. Sufism, as defined by some classic Sufi scholars, is a "science whose objective is cleansing of heart and turning it away from everything but God". Worldly possessions and the greed have to go, since you cannot serve two masters. This is a science whose practitioner can learn how to purify one's inner self from all worldly filth and spiritually ascend to be into the presence of the Divine.

Sufism developed in the 8th and 9th centuries in three major centers: 1. The cities of Basra, Kufa and Baghdad in Iraq. 2. The city of Balkh in the Khorasan district of Persia. 3. Egypt.

Muhammad is regarded as the first Sufi master who passed his esoteric teachings orally to his successors who also received his special grace (barakah). An unbroken chain of transmission of divine authority is supposed to exist from

Muhammad to his successor 'Ali and from him down to generations of Sufi masters (Sheikhs, Pirs). Each order has its own Silsilah (chain) that links it with Muhammad and 'Ali.

In Sufi way of thinking, Sufism is not owned by any faith system, religious group or sect. It manifests all the shades and colors that represent different religions and belief systems of the world and has no color of its own. By itself, it is not a religion or a philosophy, and is free of all religious sectarianism Historically, over the centuries, there have been various Sufi movements and orders. All strive to excel in self-purification and spiritual enlightenment.

If ever it was to choose a name for itself, it would be called a religion of humanity, beauty and love. A Sufi is in the presence of the Divine, every moment in life, being careful in treading through the maze of this worldly journey. There is nowhere to hide and no need to hide. At a certain point the journey is complete, and you are back to the Divine.

Sufism, or Islamic way of passing on the received knowledge, is in some ways early approach of Judaism to the subject of spirituality. This knowledge was held sacred, passed on from chest to chest and given only to those that were considered worthy of it. Sufism has been the tradition that has been the practiced by various masters, passing this knowledge down to adherents of those specific lineages. This "Given" knowledge passed down from the final messenger (PBUH) to subsequent generations

With the utmost care and instructions. Orders developed down the line, with some specificity to each order, yet the ultimate objective and the approach was essentially the same.

SUFI PRACTICE, INITIATION

Initiation into a Sufi order is seen as a necessary ritual that transmits the spiritual grace (barakah, spiritual power) of the guide (murshid) to the disciple (murid). This special grace goes back in an unbroken line to the Prophet himself. In Sufi thought it is likened to a seed planted in the initiate's soul, the equivalent of Christian baptism or new birth. At the initiation ceremony the Master who has experienced union with God and annihilation of self, in addition to giving the disciple the special garment also gives the him a secret word or prayer to help him in his meditation.

Sufis also believe in Spiritual Guides who reveal themselves to the Sufi in visions or dreams and help him on his path. Al-Khidr is one well known such guide who is sometimes identified as the prophet Elijah. The initiate has to learn spiritual poverty (faqr) which means emptying the soul of self in order to make room for God. The illusion of the individual ego must be erased by humility and love of one's neighbor. This is attained by a rigid self-discipline that removes all obstacles to the revelation of the Divine Presence. Sufism is seen as a spiritual path of self-knowledge that leads to a knowledge of God. God is seen by the "eye of the heart", not by intellectual knowledge or legalistic customs. The outward form of religion is a mere shell which hides the kernel inside it. The kernel is the truth, the Sufi's goal on his spiritual path.

The Sufi path contains many stages (Maqamat) and states (Ahwal). It begins with repentance when the seeker joins the order and prepares himself for initiation. The guide (Sheikh, Pir) accepts the seeker as his disciple by the ritual of initiation when he imparts his grace, gives him strict ascetic rules to follow and a certain secret word for meditation. The disciple's path is one of continuous struggle against his lower soul. He passes through a number of spiritual stations and states clearly defined by Sufi teaching. Following are the Sufi stations:.

1. detachment from the world (zuhd).

2. patience (sabr).

3. gratitude (shukr), for whatever God gives.

4. love (hubb).

5. pleasure (rida) with whatever God desires.

Specific moods or emotions (ahwal) are linked to these stations, such as fear and hope, sadness and joy, yearning and intimacy. Beyond this stage the Sufi then enters the state of Baqa', or perseverance in God. He returns from his state of intoxication (Sukr) back into the world completely transformed - reborn.

It is appropriate now, to mention a few lineages and orders that are present in the Islamic world today, as it relates to teachings of Sufism. It is worth remembering that these are not different forms or different teachings but rather the descendency of the given knowledge that is of interest to the disciples for their connection path to the original. Ultimate aim is the same.

SOME FAMOUS ORDERS

As of this date there are over two hundred known Sufi orders. Some are local and urban and some are global or transnational. I will mention a few:.

THE QADIRIYAH - It was founded in Baghdad by 'Abd al-Qadir Jilani (d.1166), considered to be the greatest saint in Islam, and is the oldest and most popular order. It has branches all over the world loosely tied to its center at Baghdad. It later became established in Yemen, Egypt, Sudan, the Maghreb, Central Asia and India. The Qadiriya stresses piety, humility, moderation, and philanthropy and appeals to all classes of society being strictly orthodox. It is governed by a descendant of al-Jilani who the keeper of his tomb in Baghdad is also which is a pilgrimage centre for his followers from all over the world.

THE NAQSHBANDIYA - The Naqshbandiya developed mainly as an urban order with close links to the orthodox hierarchy. They recite their Dhikr silently, ban music and dance, and prefer contemplation to ecstasy. Their "middle way" between extreme asceticism and extreme antinomianism seemed acceptable to the orthodox hierarchy. They have been involved in underground movements against Soviet rule in Central Asia and supported the Afghan Mujahedin against the Russians

This was founded in Central Asia in the thirteenth century in an attempt to defend Islam against the ravages of the Mongol invasions. It later spread to the Indian subcontinent. The Naqshbandis tried to control the political rulers so as to ensure that they implemented God's will. They were politically and culturally active, the great poet Mir Dad (d.1785) belonged to this order. They were also connected to trade and crafts guilds and held political power in the 15th century in Central Asia and in Moghul India. A Naqshbandi branch, the Khaltawiyah, had an important part in efforts to modernize the Ottoman Empire during the 18th and 19th centuries.

THE MAWLAWIYAH - The Mawlawiya were especially attractive to the educated elite of the Turkish Ottoman Empire and were widespread in Anatolia where they had close links with the authorities. This order was founded by Jalal al-Din Rumi (d.1273, called Mevlana), the greatest Sufi poet who wrote in Persian. Their rituals are aesthetically sophisticated, and their Sama' is famous for its exquisite combination of music, poetry and whirling dance (in the West they are called "Whirling Dervishes") which transports them into the trace like state.

THE BEKTASHIYA - a syncretistic order whose ritual and beliefs are a mixture of Shi'ism, Orthodox Christianity and gnostic cults. By the sixteenth century the Bektashis were the order of the famous Janissary corps, the elite military unit of the Ottoman Empire. Their magic-like rituals appealed to the illiterate masses of Anatolia. Their clergy were celibate, they practiced ritual confession and communion and had a trinitarian concept of God similar to that of the 'Alawis.

THE TIJANIYA - founded by al-Tijani in 1781 in Fez, Morocco, extended the borders of Islam towards Senegal and Nigeria and founded great kingdoms in West Africa. They taught submission to the established government and their influence is still an important factor in these countries where it is associated with conservative businessmen.

THE SUHRAWARDIYA - was started in Iraq by al-Suhrawardi (d.1234) who stressed serious training and teaching. They have many adherents in the Indian subcontinent. They were very involved politically in Iraq and Iran during the Mongol threat, seeking to ensure the survival of Islam.

THE RIFA'IYA - was founded in the marshlands of southern Iraq by al-Rifa'i (d.1187). They stress poverty, abstinence and mortification of the flesh, and are also known as the "Howling Dervishes" because of their loud recitation of the Dhikr. They focus on dramatic ritual and bizarre feats such as fire eating, piercing themselves with iron skewers and biting heads off live snakes.

THE SHADILIYA - was started by al-Shadili (d.1258) in Tunis. It flourished especially in Egypt under ibn-'Ata Allah (d.1309) but also spread to North Africa, Arabia and Syria. It is the strongest order in the Maghreb where it was organised by al-Jazuli (d. 1465) and has sub-orders under other names. The Shadiliya stress the intellectual basis of Sufism and allow their members to remain involved in the secular world. They are not allowed to beg and are always neatly dressed. They appealed mainly to the middle class in Egypt and are still active there. It is said that the Shadiliya were the first to discover the value of coffee as a means of staying awake during nights of prayer!

THE CHISHTIYA - were founded by Mu'in al-Din Chishti in Ajmer, India. His teaching was simple and the order is known for its fervour and hospitality. They helped in the islamisation of the Indian subcontinent.

SUFISM IN AMERICA

Sufism found a fertile ground for its propagation in the diverse religious landscape in America. It is important to keep in mind that the Sufi Movement seeks to remove differences and distinctions which divide us into different groups and Religions. Sufis feel that once we shed our cloak of individual religious identity, we will find that all guidance and all knowledge comes from the same, one source.

Sufism has gone through many stages in its development as a permanent spiritual tradition within the United States, and is still very multifaceted in the manner in which it is practiced and the regions of the world which American Sufi communities originate from.

The earliest introductions of Sufism to America took place in the early 1900's through scholars, writers, and artists who often accessed information on Sufism through the Orientalist movement. Examples of Western figures who were influenced by Sufism include Ralph Waldo Emerson, Rene Guenon, Reynold Nicholson, and Samuel Lewis. These individuals helped to introduce concepts of Sufism to larger audiences through their writings, discussions and other methods of influence. Emerson, for example, was influenced by Persian Sufi poetry such as that of the poet Saadi, and this influence was then reflected in Emerson's own poetry and essays. Rene Guenon incorporated information about Sufism into his traditionalist philosophy, and Nicholson offered Western readers some of the great Sufi works for the first time in the English language, especially the Mathnawi of Jelaludin Rumi.

The first major Sufi figure in the United States was Hazrat Inayat Khan, a musician from India. He blended aspects of Sufism and Islam with other spiritual, musical, and religious concepts and practices. He did not actually consider his group a Sufi group and preached a Universalist spiritual movement. Webb (1995) states: "Hazrat believed destiny had called him to speed the "universal Message of the time," which maintained that Sufism was not essentially tied to historical Islam, but rather consisted of timeless, universal teaching related to peace, harmony, and the essential unity of all being (and beings)"(p. 253). Hazrat Inayat Khan's Sufi Order in America, called 'The Sufi Order in the West' was founded in 1910. The Order continued through his disciples Rabia Martin and Samuel Lewis. Eventually Lewis broke away from the original order and began to initiate his own disciples. Similar occurrences of break-away Sufi branches and groups involving Sufi-oriented individuals such as Frithjof Schoun and Rene Geunon, Irina Tweedie and others as well as the relatives of Hazrat Inayat Khan caused the growth in different Sufi orders and communities based on individual beliefs and the blending of various Eastern and Western traditions.

Pir Vilayat Inayat Khan, the eldest son of Inayat Khan, became head of the Sufi Order in the West in 1956, after having studied in Paris and England. Both he and his father were prolific writers in English and many of the early books dealing with Sufism available in the United States were the results of their publications. Pir Vilayat wrote about the practices of meditation and other Sufi practices, music and Sufi psychology (Khan, 1993, Spiegelman, Khan & Fernandez, 1991). His father's teachings were published in many volumes by disciples. They dealt with more generalized topics dealing with spirituality, rather than specifically Sufi beliefs or ideas (Khan, 1978, Khan 1982).

The second major wave of interest in Sufism in the United States occurred in the 1960's during the hippie/counter-culture movement. Webb points out that Americans sought out Eastern teachers to learn traditional wisdom but were not concerned with the historical foundations of the traditions that were associated with that wisdom (Webb, 1995, p. 252). Figures such as Frithjof Schuon and Rene Guenon became teachers of traditional wisdom related to and sometimes directly dealing with Sufi teachings. Though these figures lived and began teaching in the earlier part of the century their teachings and writings played a larger role in the mid-twentieth century as they became available to a wider audience in the United States. Both were proponents of the traditionalist or perennial philosophy (see Guenon, 1962, 2001). Schuon (1907-1998) was a Swiss national who spent much of his time in France and published all of his major works in French. Most of his writings have now been translated into English and contribute to the body of work written in the early twentieth century that demonstrate the philosophical and spiritual thinking that emerged when East met West. Schuon was also known as Shaykh `Isa Nur al-Din Ahmad al-Shadhili alDarquwi al-`Alawi al-Maryami. He is said to have been initiated into the Shadhiliyah Sufi Order and became a leader of his own branch of the Order in the United States, known as the Maryama Order (Schuon, 1981).

Like Schuon, Rene Guenon (1886-1951) also traveled extensively and encountered various religions, eventually becoming initiated into a Sufi Order. Guenon, though a practitioner of Sufism himself, continued to write and teach from a multi-religious point of view. He never lived in the United States but from the writings of other leaders of Sufism in the west it can be seen that Guenon had a major influence on the academic community in America.

Of the Sufi groups that developed in the 1960's and 1970's some aligned themselves with Islam and traditional Sufi doctrine and practices, while others were more loosely associated with traditional Sufism and incorporated what they wanted from Sufi belief and practice into their groups. An example of a group that Godlas (2004) considers a non-Islamic Sufi group is the Sufi Ruhaniat International founded by Samuel Lewis, who was originally a disciple of Hazrat Inayat Khan. The Order claims to have members who are formally initiated students but their method of initiation and doctrinal terminology are not based on traditional Sufi doctrine. Rather, they echo the universalist ideas first put forth by Inayat Khan in the early part of the century. It was during the 60's that Lewis created Dances of Universal Peace that became known as "Sufi dancing."

Idries Shah (1924-1996) was one of the most important individuals in terms of popularizing Sufism in the United States, and perhaps still the most well known Sufi writer in the West. He began writing in the 1960's and continued to produce popular books, though he contended that Sufism was not tied to Islam or any other religion. He produced dozens of books, many of them adapting traditional Sufi stories for Western readers (Williams, 1974).

Other groups, such as the Bawa Muhaiyadeen Fellowship in the Philadelphia area, started out with little formal association with Islam but slowly moved more towards traditional Sufism and mainstream Islam. Bawa Muhaiyadeen's Sufi group is an example of a Sufi group that blended the earlier trends of Sufi practice that occurred during the 1960's and the more traditional practices that have emerged in Sufi groups today. Bawa Muhaiyadeen arrived in Philadelphia in 1971 and membership to his group, known as "the Fellowship" grew quickly and numbered nearly a thousand during his life. He lived and led his community for 15 years until his death. The community built a mosque in 1983 where congregational prayers are practiced according to Islamic law. Today, those who gather at the mosque include original converts and a large number of immigrants and non-convert Muslim Americans who do not necessarily have any allegiance to Bawa or his teachings. The teachings of Bawa were faithfully recorded, translated and published by his followers, and his teachings continue to be disseminated and gather new adherents. At the same time, part of his community has become absorbed into the greater Muslim community and is not as distinguished as a "Sufi community."

Present-day Sufi groups in the United States include groups established in the early waves of the 1920's and 1960's, and Sufi communities formed or facilitated by new immigrants to the United States who are affiliated with Sufi orders in their countries of origin. Webb asserts that some Muslim immigrants join Sufi communities in America to cultivate a deeper religiosity, or they see Sufism as an alternative to modernity. Today, many people become involved in Sufism as a contrast to the growing influence of more puritanical sects of Islam that are having growing influence on mainstream Islam.

The majority of Sufi communities in the United States are

branches of Sufi orders that exist throughout the world and originate in traditional Muslim societies. The leaders of these orders typically do not live in the United States but appoint local Shaykhs or leaders to oversee the activities of the order in America. Today nearly every Sufi order is represented in the United States either in the form of single or multiple communities throughout the country or by visiting/traveling Shaykhs of an order. There are at least a dozen Sufi orders with larger communities established in the United States.

Examples of Sufi orders that have established communities in the United States are the Jerrahiyyah Order of dervishes, the Naqshbandi, the Mevlevi Order, the Nimatullahi Order, the Tijani Order and the Qadiriyyah Order. The Naqshbandi Order is represented by a very large community in the United States under the Naqshbandi-Haqqani group established by Shaykh Nazim. The Order is run by Shaykh Hisham Kabbani, a Middle Eastern man who has grown to be an international figure representing American Sufis in his travels throughout the world. He came to the United States in 1991 and has established thirteen Sufi centers throughout the United States and Canada. The Chishti Order is a major Sufi Order of South Asia that has also become established with several branches operating throughout the United States and Canada. The Nimatullahi Order is also well-established in the United States due to its leader, Dr. Javad Nurbakhsh, who has published dozens of books in the English language on topics ranging from basic Sufi practices, Sufi symbolism, and Sufi psychology. The Order also publishes a magazine in both English and Persian called Sufi: A Journal of Sufism. Despite Rumi being one of the most important figures as far as exposing Sufi concepts to the West in the last several decades, his order is represented in the United States not in its traditional form, but rather as a Quasi-Islamic Sufi Organization as the term is described by Godlas (2004).

Some of the Sufi communities are loosely linked and meet sporadically. Others are very tightly formed communities that actively practice aspects of their daily lives in a community form. Some Sufi communities, such as the Bawa Muhayiadden Fellowship, maintain their own printing presses.

One cannot discuss Sufism in America without mentioning some of the major academic figures over the last half-century who have, through their writing or teaching, influenced American Sufism in many ways. Several individuals in university settings have played an important role in spreading information on Sufism to a large student population, popularizing Sufism amongst younger generations of Americans.

Seyyed Hossein Nasr and Victor Danner are amongst an older generation of professors whose teachings in American University settings have helped to shape the American understanding of Sufism. Nasr, originally the minister of education in Iran before the Iranian revolution has taught in several institutional settings and is the author of dozens of books and articles in multiple languages dealing with Sufism and Sufi topics. His involvement in bringing hundreds of young students into the folds of Sufism cannot be underestimated. Victor Danner, who was born in Mexico in 1926 and earned his PhD from Harvard University after having served as a young man in World War II. He taught at Indiana University for more than two decades in the subjects of Sufism, Islam, mysticism, as well as the Arabic language. He authored a few books and many articles which have contributed to the available literature of Sufism, and his courses dealing with Sufism were extremely popular throughout the 1970's and 1980's. <u>Three other scholars who, though not American or teachers in American schools, who have had a strong impact on American Sufism, include Martin Lings, Titus Burckhardt, and Annemarie Schimmel</u>. There is little biographical information available for either Lings or Burckhardt who lived fairly private lives and are best known for their writings in English dealing with Sufism. Burckhardt was a Swiss who followed the Traditionalist school, and his writings and essays touched on Sufism. Lings is the former Keeper of Oriental manuscripts in the British Museum and Library, and has authored several famous and acclaimed books dealing with Islamic Mysticism as well as a biography of the Prophet Muhammad.

Annemarie Schimmel, a German scholar and linguist, authored more than fifty books dealing with Islam, Sufism and South Asian topics. She was an expert in Islamic mysticism and her books are extremely popular in the United States. All three scholars' writings are of major importance for American and other Western students of Sufism, and continue to be authoritative texts for those interested in Sufism, Islam, and mysticism in general.

Hermansen (2000) points out that little attention has been given to Sufi movements in America because they have not been considered a significant population in terms of the overall Muslim community. She uses the term movement to describe Sufi groups. The term community or group will be used rather than movement because the term movement often implies an underlying political or reformist connection, which is rarely a part of Sufi communities in America.

Gabbay (1988) also gives a description of the history and development of Sufism, including Sufism's introduction to American. More importantly he offers a description of American Sufi practitioners in which one hundred and thirty-one practitioners filled out a survey measuring their level of involvement with Sufism and the impact of Sufism on their lives. These types of studies are leading to a greater understanding of the history and place of Sufism in the American spiritual landscape.

Hermansen points out that there are a number of movements that are Sufi-oriented or influenced by Islamic mysticism but which do not follow the practice of Islamic law. She refers to these types of Sufi movements as perennial because they stress the unity of religions and do not usually require the formal practice of Islam by their members. Both perennial Sufi groups and more traditionalist Sufi groups continue to exist in the United States, and many of them maintain relationships with each other despite their differences in doctrine.

Godlas (2004) refers to three main categories of Sufism in the United States; Islamic Sufi Orders, Quasi-Islamic Sufi organizations, and Non-Islamic Sufi organizations. This is an accurate description of Sufi groups in the United States over the past century and demonstrates the difficulty of examining the practices of Sufi groups due to the differences in level of traditional doctrines.

William Chittick and his wife Sachiko Murata, both former students of Nasr, Bruce Lawrence and Carl Ernst in North Carolina, Alan Godlas in Georgia, and Laleh Bakhtiar in Illinois, as well as dozens of others spread throughout the country at numerous colleges, universities, and other intellectual and professional institutions. This younger generation of scholars and research are impacting American Sufis and Sufi communities through their ability to reach large audiences of non-Sufis in the academic environment and for their prolific work in translating Sufi works and publishing on topics of Sufism in the English language.

The differences in beliefs, doctrines, and practices of the Sufi communities in the United States makes it very hard for those outside of these communities to define or group them in one way. The contentiousness the authenticity of Sufi groups in the United States by some Sufis also has made it hard for those not involved with communities to understand the role of Sufism in general in the United States, because there are many different types of Sufism being practiced in these communities. All these types of communities, and the beliefs and practices which they have incorporated into their group are of importance to the history of Sufism in the United States and the continuing growth of the tradition in the West.

Chapter 17

.... One and the same
Message:

The Islamic perspective of life as recorded in the history tells us that all of us have descended from Adam, who was created by the Almighty God out of Clay. The creator breathed his spirit into Adam and ordered him to be, and he was. All of us have descended from one Adam and his mate Eve that was created from Adam to be his companion. Human race started from this one couple. Adam was the first prophet of God. For every community there have been chosen human beings who were given the high status of being Divine Messengers. It was the messengers a job to receive revelations from the creator and transmit them and implement them on the people that lived in their communities. Naturally earlier prophets had smaller communities to guide and to convey the message of God for a just and coherent society. As humans increased there were multiple profits in different areas of the globe basically giving the same message to humanity about the existence of God, creation of universe and the purpose of human life. All these prophets taught humans to be fair and just to each other believe in one God worship only him and no one else. And believe that they will be judged one day after death for whatever they have done during their lifetime. This concept of the day of judgment after death was common in all the divinely revealed religions.

In the earlier times humans were incapable of transmitting the word of God down to the next generations by any means other than the word of mouth. Societies in various parts of the globe did start to write few generations down from Adam, but there were no resources or means to preserve the written word. Humans did write on stones on the walls of the caves and made some figures that stayed after their death for some years, but the future generations did not always understand these writings or their meaning.

It took several centuries for humans to develop languages that could be written and the material like paper to be able to record their experiences. Message of our creator has been the same throughout the centuries of human history. Basically, we are to believe in one God worship him alone consider him to be all-knowing and all seeing. We have to realize that one day after death, we will be resurrected and will be held accountable for what we have done in our lives. The concept of punishment for those who have done wrong and rewarding those who have been right and God-fearing is common to all the Divine religions. Descriptions may vary but we are advised to be just to each other be fair in our dealings with others and help each other in our lives.

One might ask why it is then that for last 1400 plus years we have not received any new prophets. The easy answer to this question is "God knows best", but there is another amazingly simple and plausible answer. Now we have with us, the original message of God, in his own original words, unaltered and unedited by man. This message is for the entire humanity and for all times to come. This revealed book "Al-Qura'an", came to our final messenger through Angel Gabriel and in Arabic language fourteen hundred plus years ago. This message for humanity that took 23 years to complete, and is memorized by millions of humans. The Almighty himself says in this book, "Undoubtedly we have sent down this book and we alone are the protectors of it." Since this message is in its original form, protected, unedited by humans, and is relevant to our future generations, the mission is complete. The creator's message to humanity is clear as it testifies to the authenticity of the message in the original languages of the prior revealed books. God intended only one message for the creation, total submission to him and him alone. You can call it by any name in any language but in Arabic, it will be called "Islam".

Why then this message has not been accepted and welcomed by the entire humanity? Is it by design that we are all programmed to adhere to and to hold onto what we have and not accept any change? Is this the test and ongoing challenge for us all that is part of an overall design of life on Earth? Simple answer, once again, is "God only knows", and of course, "God knows best".

If one studies spirituality with an open and inquisitive mind, it becomes quite apparent that, all of us "Humans" in our makeup, are quite similar and one and the same. As we trace our steps back to the times gone bye, we start to realize that our paths start to converge. That convergence leads us eventually to a common path that seems to be coming out of the same point. The abode of the Divine or the "House of Truth". Once we get to that house of the Truth, we realize that the Truth is one and the same for all. The Almighty gave the same message to humanity through

162

his messengers and we all should be following the same path in life.

There is one factor that comes into play when we try to understand the reality of that "Truth". That seems to explain why we have several versions of the Truth in the world. Each version believed by its adherents to be the true and authentic version. That factor according to my understanding, is the nature of the realm of the Divine. We humans, by our nature, are incapable of comprehending that realm. Our intellect is finite and cannot grasp the infinite. Scriptures tell us that again and again. Despite all this, our intellect does fill in the blanks, each sect in its own way, and thus our understandings are different when it comes to minor details. Big picture by and large is similar in most religions and points to the same deity. Why would the Almighty, that one God, give different messages to different messengers and create many religions when he is one and all of us are created by him. The purpose of our being is to be his representatives on earth and serve his creation.

Does anyone really believe that the Almighty wanted to create different religions by design, to keep us in separate groups or societies. Of course not. The names that we are known by i.e. Buddhism, Hinduism, Judaism, Christianity etc. are the names that we have designed by ourselves. Call me biased but there is only one name given to the religion by the creator that is still in its original language, original words, and in its original form. That name is Islam. Literally translated, it means total submission to the creator. It is not "Mohammedanism". The Prophet of Islam

(PBUH) did not make up that name or bring this religion to the world. It was sent from the Divine, brought by angel Gabriel and is the same religion that was given to all the preceding prophets beginning with Adam. It does not negate any of the teachings of the prior divine faith systems, but rather authenticates them. No one can claim to be a Muslim unless he or she has a firm belief in all the prior divine books and the prophets. Central theme in the Divine message is "Oneness of God" and the belief in the unseen".

Muslims believe in purity and innocence of all Prophets and Messengers of God and consider them to be specially chosen humans and regard them equally in high reverence. They are not to be considered like ordinary people. Their actions in the world were divinely inspired and hence beyond our critique. Finding fault in the deeds of any of the Divine Messengers is against the teachings of faith.

No one can claim to be a Muslim unless he or she has a firm belief in all the prior divine books and the prophets. Central theme in the Divine message is "Oneness of God" and the belief in the unseen". Muslims believe in purity and innocence of all Prophets and Messengers of God and consider them to be specially chosen humans and regard them equally in high reverence. They are not to be considered like ordinary people. Their actions in this worldly life, were divinely inspired, the will of God and hence beyond our critique. Finding fault in the deeds of any of the Divine Messengers is against the teachings of faith.

....   Today's man is on a slippery slope of declining humanity as he advances in science and technology. He has made no positive change in himself but is permanently changing his world to his own detriment. I am afraid, he is making himself irrelevant to his surroundings and is closer to his own decay than he realizes.

Chapter 18

"The real problem is in the hearts and minds of men. It is easier to denature plutonium than to denature the evil spirit of man." .... (Albert Einstein)

Have A Life   ....

Our time on earth is limited and whatever time we have, is a precious commodity. We must value this commodity and spend it wisely. Most of us "go" through life, rather than "grow" through life. For the growth to take place, we have to realize that we must not be totally lost in pursuit of material possessions and must "learn as we earn". We are rich only if we are blessed with the things that money cannot buy. Money is good to have and there is nothing wrong in striving to acquire it, but it should not be the only objective in life. Good health, a loving family, respect in the eyes of others, loyal friends, inner peace and happiness – these are the assets that cannot be ordered online or purchased in the marketplace. We must be cognizant of the value of these assets and try to acquire and preserve them.

We should not live to see the day that we are so poor - so poor - that all we have is money.

The Human Potential:

Man is created in the image of God. All of us have an innate potential to do things that are extraordinary and inconceivable in ordinary circumstances. The spark in each one of us that gives us life has come from the divine and has divine powers that spark is not present in all of us in the same major does who recognize this potential and nurture it by living their lives in a certain way, nurtured this potential so that it manifests its powers. Motor one concentrates on developing this potential stronger this innate power becomes. This innate spark resides in our heart. Rather, it resides in our chest and is nourished by certain actions and is certain lifestyle. Islamic philosophy of life describes this innate structure as the true self. Often individual. This entity resides in the spiritual heart that houses human soul. As the soul is awakened nurtured through good deeds and through remembrance of its true origin, it starts to grow in its potential man who possesses this awakened soul starts to manifest certain qualities and capabilities that ordinary humans do not. There is nothing impossible for a person who has purified soul residing in his heart that has been nurtured in a particular way. Such are the people who do God's work on earth and can be seen at many places at the same time. Our intellect finds it very hard to believe that's why most of us simply walk on by, as we hear about things like this and reject it out of hand as imagination of some individuals without a basis in fact.

The holy Scriptures of Islam. Al-Qura'n says that a true believer who lives a pious God-fearing life is a helper of God. He does God's work on earth and keeps his special identity hidden from common people. Many a time, such individuals may be seen performing certain activities or actions that may look hard and outright improper toward another individual. What is the real purpose behind such actions is only known to God and could manifest itself at some future date. The Scriptures give the story of such a pious man who is not a prophet that lived at the time off prophet Moses.

Moses one day just reflecting on his life and his nearness to God was thinking within himself that, is there anyone on this earth, now, that is more close to God then myself. Then he was inspired to walk to an area where two rivers meet very well find such a person. Curious as he was. Moses walked to that area and he came upon an individual who is not named in the Scripture but is thought to be Khizr. As prophet Moses recognized this individual to be close to God, he identified himself to his and was told that he must accompany him but not ask any questions. Moses promised and agreed to be patient and observant without interfering in anything that he witnesses.

As they walked, they came upon the riverbank and summoned a boat to cross the river. As the owner of the boat took them to the other, this man damaged the bottom of the boat and disabled it. Moses could not help himself and asked why he did that and why would he damage someone's personal property and cause them distress and personal loss. Moses was told to be patient and not ask any questions and walk along. He was reminded of the promise that he made at the beginning of the journey not to question anything that he witnesses. Moses apologized and started to walk along.

As they both moved on, they passed by a village. They

asked some village folk for some food and were denied. As they were leaving, Moses broke down the boundary wall of a house and continued onward without giving any reason as to why he was destroying someone's private property. Once again. Moses got very upset with that and he said that he saw no reason why you would breakdown someone's wall. Once again Moses reminded to be patient and not question anything that was happening before him.

Sometime later they came upon a young lad who was joyfully playing by himself. Moses walked up to him and for no apparent reason, murdered him. Moses could not stand it and demanded to know as to why did he take an innocent life.?

Upon hearing this, the man stopped and said this is enough. We can no longer walk together, and this final question was the last straw on the camel's back. Now we must part company but before you go. Let me tell you what why I did what I did in the past few instances.

I broke the boat that belonged to two hard-working young boys who needed this boat to earn a living. They were supporting a family and needed this boat for themselves. I temporarily disabled this boat, realizing full well that the boys will be able to repair it in a few days and make it functional again. But for now, the board will be disabled and useless. Kings men are coming this way and they would have taken away all the functioning boats for their own use and these poor people will lose their boat forever. The reason I knocked down that wall of that house was because under that wall is a treasure buried that was left by the owner of that house for his children. At the time the treasure was buried, these children were very young and small and could not have handled it. Now that they had grown once they rebuild tthis wall, they will discover that treasure and will be able to use it for their needs. And finally that teenager that was murdered by me was to save his parents from the disgrace and the shame that he would've brought to them by his deeds. It was destined that the integrity and honesty and respect of this family is not destroyed by this young individual, so it was God's will that he be removed from the scene. There are deeper purposes behind the actions. But suffice it to say that things are not necessarily what they appear to be to most people.

In this narration, one learns that there may be ordinary looking people walking the streets who may have been given responsibilities or powers, seemingly greater than those given the prophets. This man was not a prophet, and yet he had a thing or two to teach Moses. Similarly, a man, a courtier of King Soloman, who brought before King Solomon, the throne of Queen Sheba was not a prophet but had tremendous powers given to him by the Almighty God. That story from Al-Qura'n is an interesting one and is worth recounting here to illustrate this point.

Scripture tells us that King Soloman had a mighty kingdom and ruled over a large part of land and many creations of God. He could understand the language of many creatures including the birds and insects. The wind was also under his command. He lived quite a long life. One day, the woodpecker was late in arriving in his court session and King Soloman was unhappy about his carelessness in not being on time. As the woodpecker arrived, he narrated the story of a wealthy Queen who was a ruler in a faraway land and had a magnificent throne of precious metals, inlaid with precious Gemstones. King Solomon became curious and wanted to see that throne. He asked his courtiers, which amongst you can bring that throne here, for me to see. A Jinn stood up and said that I am trustworthy and can bring that throne here in time before we disperse from this meeting. A man, with the knowledge from "The Book" stood up and said, "I can bring it here in the blink of an eye". When King Solman saw the throne right in front of him, he was at awe with the beauty and the grandeur of the throne. He immediately proclaimed, "This is due to the Grace of my Creator". An ordinary looking man had this extraordinary ability to bring an object weighing many tons, from thousands of miles, almost in no time. Such is the mighty power of our creator, and he can give such power to any of his servants. The points to ponder are, how come King Soloman did not know about this man before. Also how was this man so sure that he made such an assertion. How come this man had more power in such matters than King Soloman who was a mighty ruler of his time.

The point to note in this story is that when our creator mad man as his viceregent or "Khalifa" on earth, he did place this potential in man to be able to do extraordinary things. Prophets are chosen people and have a high status but that does not mean that ordinary looking people do not have the potential for such feats. When an ordinary looking man decides to seek closeness to the creator and starts on the path of spiritual cleansing, he or she can travel this path based on the conviction and the pure intention. We are told that if we walk one step towards Him with sincerity, he walks ten steps towards us. A stage comes in this process when He, the Creator becomes our hands that we touch by, He becomes our eyes that we see with, and he becomes our feet that we walk by. Not that our creator has hands, eyes or feet but that our own faculties draw from his power, and he does his work through us. Alas, if man only knew who he is and what he is capable of.

Chapter 19

......Use your senses to gather information. Receive the data with
an open mind.
Let your inner self guide you to "The Truth"

After all is said and done,
we are similar,
We are one.

***

Descended from same ancestors, we have the same genetic makeup and similar biologic existence. Spreading around the globe over the millenniums, we have evolved to survive in our different and unique environments. Weather patterns that we were exposed to, and our other variable survival needs , have molded us into recognizably different groups and families. Our physical body has been subjected to many variables, causing us to manifest certain skin colors and bodily features for a better survival. Our soul however, has been unaffected and has been the same. Our innate nature, our instinctive behavior, and our quest to know the truth is the same in all of us.

Now that we have traversed this Earth "full circle" and this Earth is being recognized as a mere "Global Village", our coming together is not only inevitable but necessary. It is time to recognize that our survival heretofore depends on recognizing ourselves and thus shedding off all the biases we have had about each other in the past. We always shared the same water and same air but now we share the same airwaves and the same world wide web. The distances have vanished. We are now much closer to each other than we realize. Let us acknowledge it.

Our ancestors, in centuries past, may have destroyed or decimated certain tribes or villages during the times of strife between them but they had no ability to annihilate each other. We, in twenty first century, do. Our technological advances and the acquisition of nuclear arsenal, leaves us no choice but to sit together and talk. We must recognize the Human Family as one, for our own sake. Our future and our survival depend on it.Central to our survival as a species and our planning a secure and safe future is our ability of self-realization. Once we come to terms with the reason of our being and the purpose of our lives, we will be more mindful of our need and our respect for each other. This life is but a miniscule part of our actual existence.

We come into this world, pure with a Divine spark in us. The seat of that spark, metaphorically speaking, is in our Heart. We have the innate ability to keep that spark alive, cleanse the heart and see the true nature of ourselves and God. The worldly experience has the potential to pollute our heart and take us away from knowing ourselves and God. Our challenge is to make it through the journey of life by recognizing our true nature and living out the purpose of our journey of this world. Most of us go through life being totally oblivious to our true nature and having a biologic survivalist existence. Some find the true purpose of life and become agents of God as his true helpers and viceregents in this world.

Chapter 20

.... An organized and purposeful day builds a
beautiful life.

My "7-S" Formula.

SEVEN SECRETS FOR SUCCESS

1. **SMILE.** Don't forget to wear your smile every day before you wear anything else. It is under your full control, forever clean and ready to wear, always matches with anything else you wear and above all it is free. It brings out your best face for the world and it is miraculously infectious. People can't help but feel happy to see you. It is the charity you give others for being alive, well, and ready for a good day. It opens your world for you and people feel at ease approaching you and working with you. Nature has yet to bring out a better dress for mankind than a beautiful smile.

2. **SELF / SOLITUDE.** Whatever else you do in your twenty-four-hour day, save some time exclusively for yourself. Disconnect yourself from your surroundings. Relax and take a few deep breaths. No phone calls, TV, or any other distraction. Twenty to thirty minutes every day is usually enough. This is your personal time to reflect

upon yourself, analyze your life, think what you learnt from your past twenty-four hours and how you can organize your next twenty-four hours. Make things happen rather than let them happen. Do the self-analysis and the learn the art of self-accountability. Have you been fair to your family, your work and the people that you interact with - your associates?

3. **STUDY.** You must stay connected to the world around you by staying in touch with it. The world speaks to you through the literature, periodical journals, and the newspapers. Set some time apart from your daily schedule for studying the best sellers of your time and the old classics. This relaxes your mind, enriches you intellectually and equips you to be a good participant in any social setting. It builds self-confidence. If you happen to be a writer, a poet, or in any other field of fine arts, this is the time that can trigger, cultivate and nurtures that creative ability.

4. **SWEAT.** Daily exercise is a must for a sense of wellbeing and a healthy long life. Depending on the stage of life and other health related issues, one sets aside appropriate time for putting every part of the body to use. Twenty minutes to half hour daily is minimum that one should allocate. Start with simple stretching and then turn to your exercise routine based on your time availability and health conditions. Elderly can choose to start with few

deep breaths, simple stationary stretching followed by gentle walk on level ground, up to tolerance. The idea is to keep the heart and the lungs fully operational and to use all muscles and organs of the body in an organized and ongoing basis. This avoids weakness due to disuse atrophy. Medical studies have shown that if you put athletes and bodybuilders in their mid-twenties, at the prime of their health, to full bed rest for 30 days except to sit up to eat and use the toilet facilities, they lose over twenty five percent of their functional capability. Staying physically active and regular exercise is helpful in maintaining good physical health. This might be the Divine wisdom behind the obligatory five daily prayers practiced by Muslims.

5. **SLEEP.** Body needs a good restful sleep to recharge itself and be ready for the next day. Night sleep is most restful since it is synchronous with nature. Early to bed and early to rise is the best rule in life. It is recommended that one must get to bed only to sleep and not to enjoy snacks or watch television. An adult's body needs about seven to eight hours of sleep on an average and children need about ten hours. Some people can train their bodies to function well even with four to six hours of daily sleep but that is an exception. Rising early and having a couple of hours for yourself in the morning is unquestionably a secret of happiness and success. Your body and mind is at its best at the time and there is very

little disturbance in the environment. You begin your activities on time and are never late or unprepared for the day.

6. **SINCERITY.** Be true to yourself. Choose the field or vocation in life that you are borne for. Everyone has a special liking and talent that in his or her nature. Choose the field that you are attracted to and not the one that you think pays you most. Do not continue to work where you are unhappy and feel out of place. Put your best effort in whatever you do and be sincere to yourself and your job. Take the day seriously and prove up to the task. This forces you to perform optimally and shine amongst your peers. If you perform up to the expectations, the world is waiting for you to move you up the ladder. Remember, you are being compared to your peers. You need to be a little bit better than others around you and next thing you know, you are selected for promotion and have moved up the ladder. Selecting the right vocation in life and sincerity with your job description can give tremendous happiness in life. If you enjoy your work, you are basically on vacation all your life. You can't wait to come to work. People can have an easy life and get bye, doing little as possible and seemingly enjoying all the benefits of the job but all they do is deprive themselves of realizing their full potential. They have never known real happiness or the satisfaction that comes with extraordinary achievements.

7. **SUPPLICATE.** This is my favorite and that is why I have kept it for the last. Regardless of whether you believe in any faith system or not, you are borne with a certain innate feeling about some higher authority that runs your universe. Learn to appreciate what you have in your life and be thankful for it. Without any effort on your part, you got millions of gifts including your physical body, your health, your intelligence, and your family. Be thankful for it. Learn to find reasons to thank your parents, your siblings, your children, and your co-workers on a regular basis. Acknowledging something good in others is a way of thanking them for being a part of your life. If you are a believer in a faith system, pray and connect to your creator to be thankful for all the blessings in your life. He is there to give you more if you sincerely ask. The Peace of mind that you get in that communication can be beyond measure. Be thankful, always fore whatever you have in life because it can be taken away also as easily as it came. Learning to be thankful to others opens a way for others to appreciate you for what you have. And remember, what goes around, comes around.

Recommended Reading

Main source is The Holy Scriptures, The Torah, Bible and Al-Qura'n.

1. Alchemy of Happiness.
   (Al-Ghazali, Abu-Hamid)
2. A History of God.
   (Karen Armstrong)
3. God, Faith and Reason
   (Michael Savage)
4. Masnavi-e-Maanavi.
   (Mevlana Jalal ud Din Rumi)
5. Divan-e Shams-e-Tabrizi.
   (Mevlana Jalal ud Din Rumi)
6. Conversations with God.
   (Neale Donald Walsch)
7. How to awaken the power within you.
   (Diana Dolice)
8. The Sufi Doctrine of Rumi.
   (William C. Chittick)
9. Sapiens.
   (Yuval Noah Harari)
10. Spirituality simplified.
    (Jeff Maziareck)
11. The Lives of Men
    (Imam A.I.A Haddad
12. Islamic philosophy... to present.
    (Seyyed Hossein Nasr)

RECEIVE & GIVE

Universe is constantly in motion, rotating and expanding.

All the Heavenly Bodies are in a very orderly spin.

Earth rotates on its axis and around the sun.

(A Whirling Dervish)

So, like a whirling Dervish, Synchronize yourself with your Universe.

Turn your right hand up and receive from the Divine.

Turn your left hand down to give to His creation.

Look inwards, spin, and get connected

with the Universe & The Divine.

***

Printed in Great Britain
by Amazon

75189540R00104